To Desi

From Lauraine

14/2/01.

PORSCHE

PORSCHE

GENERATIONS OF GENIUS

Brian Laban

GREENWICH EDITIONS

This edition published 2000 by
Greenwich Editions
10 Blenheim Court
Brewery Road
London N7 9NT

© Chrysalis Books 2000
A member of the Chrysalis Group plc

ISBN 0-86288-385-7

ACKNOWLEDGEMENTS
The editor is grateful to the individual owners and companies who allowed
their Porsches to be photographed for this book. In Germany, of paramount importance
has been the contribution of Dr. Ing. h.c.F. Porsche Aktiengesellschaft,
Stuttgart–Zuffenhausen, which gave access to a substantial number of cars in its
museum's collection. Especial thanks go to Herr Klaus Parr for the time
and generosity and expertise he devoted to the project, and to
Herr Peter Schneider and Herr Rolf Koch of the Porsche museum.
Herr Bodo Neumann, Dr Hans Luipold and Herr Wolfgang Striffler
also offered assistance. In France, M. Patrick Garnier and M. Pierre-Jean Remy,
Musée National de l'Automobile, Collection Schlumpf, Mulhouse,
gave help with two cars on exhibit in the museum. In England, thanks are also due to
the following, without whose contributions it would have been difficult to proceed:
John and Susan Cleave (Portia Cars Ltd), Roy Gillham (Porsche Club of Great Britain),
Claire Knee and Christine Long (Porsche Cars GB), Nick and Jane Lancaster
(Lancaster Porsche, Colchester), Dominic Lancaster (Lancaster Porsche, Bow),
the Midland Motor Museum, Howard Pitts, Philip Spani (Lancaster Porsche, Bow),
Bill Stephens, Michael Ticehurst. Most of the photographs appearing in this book
were taken by Janus van Helfteren and Ian Kuah. The photographs on pages 160–75
were kindly supplied by Porsche UK and the LAT Photographic Library.

Production by Omnipress, Eastbourne
Printed in Italy

CONTENTS

INTRODUCTION

The words genius and classic may be over-used in motoring life, but if they can genuinely be said to apply anywhere, they most certainly apply to successive generations of the Porsche family, and to the cars they have built – outstanding individuals and outstanding creations even in the world of supercars.

Ferdinand Porsche, founder of the dynasty, was born in 1875 and was working with cars even before the turn of the century. He was sometimes a racing driver, sometimes a designer of aero engines and military high technology, but always a pioneer. In the early 1920s he designed a small sporty car for Austro-Daimler, known as the Sascha; he worked as designer at Daimler, as chief engineer at Steyr and then late in 1930 he set up his own design bureau in Stuttgart, which became the basis of the modern Porsche empire.

Starting with Project number 7, because he didn't want any customer to think that he was the first, Porsche designed cars as diverse as the V W Beetle – Hitler's 'people car' – and the awesome mid-engined Auto-Union GP cars of the late 1930s. In 1932 the Russian government invited him to inspect their industry and discuss terms for becoming their 'State Designer', with the promise of almost limitless resources. But he declined – as disinclined to become involved in Russian politics as he would later be towards being drawn into Nazi ones.

His reluctance to be drawn into the political side of Germany's war effort was one thing however; his designs for everything from V W-engined generators to some of the war's finest tanks was

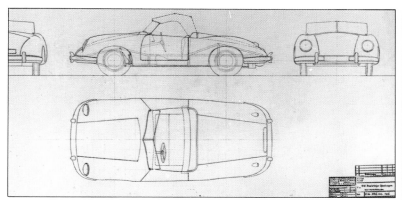

The beginning: 1947 drawings for 356-1 . . .

. . . and the first car.

strictly another, and when he was invited to France at the end of the war, ostensibly to design another 'people's car', he soon found himself in jail, with son Ferry and son-in-law Dr Anton Piëch, husband of his daughter, Louise. He was accused of war-time collaboration, and although it became increasingly clear that the charges had no substance, the French would hold Professor Porsche and Dr Piëch until August 1947. Ferry, on the other hand, had been released by mid-1946, and having returned to Austria he joined Louise in Gmünd, where she had kept the design bureau running with determination and considerable courage.

And design work was the key to Professor Porsche's ultimate release from his dubious French internment, the 'bail' that the authorities demanded finally being earned from the design of the outstandingly advanced, if ultimately abortive Cisitalia GP car for the wealthy Italian industrialist, Piero Dusio.

By the time Professor Porsche was released, his health was poor, but his intellect and his ambition were as intense as ever; and, perhaps knowing that time was now likely to be short, he had one ambition in particular. In 1948, back in Gmünd, he finally committed himself to building sports cars under his own name, starting with the VW-based project number 356.

The first Porsche, with a mid-mounted engine and open, roadster bodywork, was completed early in 1948, in works which were little more than a large shed in what was once a wood yard but which had now become a busy Porsche operation for repairing other people's

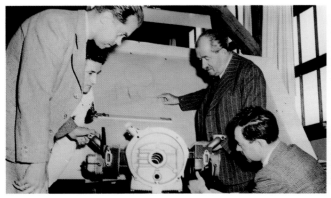

Professor Porsche (standing, right) with Ferry (kneeling).

Ferry and thriving 356 line at Zuffenhausen.

broken vehicles. Later in 1948 Porsche built the first coupé version of the 356 (with a rear engine) and the pattern was set for Porsches right up to the present day.

With modest power, the 356 paid utmost attention to light weight, excellent chassis behaviour and exceptional aerodynamics, just as the V W had; as such, it had performance way beyond what its modest power and utility-car inheritance might have suggested – and people recognised that to such a degree that Porsche's early production estimates proved wildly short of the mark.

What was good for performance on the road was good for racing too, and with due consideration Porsche came to the conclusion that being involved in motor sport could only be good for them. In 1951, the first Porsche appeared at Le Mans. It was a lightweight version of one of the very first Gmünd-built 356 coupés and, driven by Porsche's French distributor, it comfortably won its class, setting the scene for a competition history virtually without equal for the Porsche marque.

Racing also gave Porsche one of its great model names, when a more potent version of the 356 was named for Porsche's success in the Carrera Panamericana, and the Carrera line has run through Porsche history ever since. And as well as becoming faster and having better handling, Porsches have also become far more civilised and sophisticated than the basic 356s could ever have been. When the second generation was launched, in the guise of the 911, one of Ferry Porsche's design parameters was that it should have the

911: the second Porsche legend.

Latest generation: the 968.

space to carry a full set of golf clubs, while still being unashamedly a sports car – because that alone was what Porsche built. It did all that could have been asked of it, and astonishingly, almost thirty years later the latest 911s are still at the very core of Porsche's success.

What it also did, though, was to move the mainstream Porsche product into a higher price and sophistication bracket than in the days of the 356, and that in turn opened the way for a whole series of attempts to create a lower priced, higher volume model, usually in collaboration with VW, who were still a powerful ally well into the 1970s. And Porsche purists may scorn the 'lesser' models like the 912, the 914 and 924, but they are every bit as much a part of the Porsche story as the archetypal rear-engined 356s and 911s – just as the front-engined 928, 944 and now the 968 models are towards the other end of the price scale.

The simple fact is that Porsches arouse strong emotions, from the die-hards who insist that the only true Porsche has an air-cooled flat engine behind the rear wheels, to the pragmatists who take Porsche's own admirable attitude and reckon that nothing should be considered impossible. So the pursuit of excellence in every area remains, and the twenty-five cars that follow tell the story of how the company has grown around it. The majority of them are road cars, some of them, inevitably, have a racing purpose too. They run right through to the 450bhp of the ultra-sophisticated, limited-edition, four-wheel-drive 959, and the Le Mans winning 935, via the current 320bhp 911 Turbo and the newest generation, the 968.

356 ROADSTER

By the middle of 1947, the Porsche design bureau had reached project number 356, but although every design to date had borne the unmistakable hallmark of Porsche's genius, not one of those projects so far had been a car bearing Porsche's own name. Project 356 was about to correct that situation.

When the drawings were officially started, on 17 July 1947, the design office (having been moved from Stuttgart towards the end of the war) was in temporary exile in Gmünd, on the edge of the mountains in the far south of Austria. Professor Ferdinand Porsche was still held by the French, on the dubious charges levelled at him at the end of the war. In his absence, his son Ferry, now in his late thirties and himself only released from brief internment in July 1946, was keeping the business running. In setting up the deal for Porsche to design the Cisitalia GP car (for Italian industrialist Piero Dusio), he had generated the funds to help release his father from almost two years of detention.

In August 1947, Professor Porsche was freed, and headed straight back to Gmünd and the early planning stages of the car that would finally carry his name. Physically he was weak, but he had lost none of his genius for original thinking, and although Ferry and the faithful chief designer Karl Rabe had already done much of the basic work, Professor Porsche still had plenty to contribute.

In fact, to a great extent Ferdinand Porsche had sown the seeds for his own marque's future even before the war, when he created the V W Beetle, and it was that car which was the natural starting point for the first true Porsche, in more ways than one would have expected.

Porsche's first stroke of good fortune was that the V W had survived the war at all, with the almost totally ruined factory being rebuilt and put back to work under British military auspices during 1945. It even managed to produce a little over 900 cars by the end of that year. That would at least mean that the basic building blocks around which Project 356 was being planned still existed, though that didn't necessarily mean they were readily available. On the contrary, in the early days the tiny operation in Gmünd (working in what amounted to not much more than a large wood yard) used a mixture of parts

The unique mid-engined layout of 356-1 made the cockpit (right) a strict two-seater, with no space behind the seats. The philosophy of highly efficient aerodynamics to offset lack of power was clear from the start, in the Roadster's unsullied, ultra-smooth lines, with tucked-under sills (overleaf).

Under the simple rear hatch, which didn't even have a cooling grille (below), the V W-derived engine was set ahead of the four-speed gearbox, which also changed the V W rear suspension from trailing to leading link, and led to problems with the torsion bar mountings.

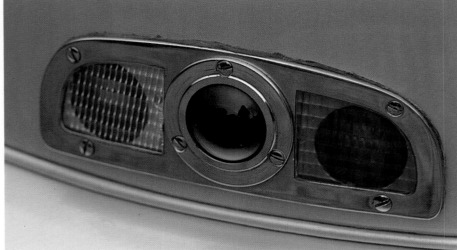

that had survived from the original development and ones 'liberated' with various degrees of negotiation and ingenuity from the factory.

Project 356 would use a VW engine, transmission, suspension, brakes and steering, as well as many smaller items. And that was a matter of philosophy as well as of expediency. Professor Porsche's brief when designing the 'Beetle' had been to build a car with ambitious performance and durability targets, but down to a seemingly impossible price; by original thinking and his genius for simplification, Porsche came far closer to the brief than any other engineer had ever thought possible, and what held for the Beetle would hold equally well for the 356.

Of course, Porsche simply didn't *have* access to anything more powerful than the air-cooled flat-four VW engine, so they would have to save weight and make the car as aerodynamic as possible in compensation. The VW itself had done much the same: the engine was at the back to minimise the weight and cost of driveline components; it was air-cooled to save the weight and cost of radiators, pipes and water; it was shaped to make the most of its meagre power on Hitler's planned autobahn network; and light weight even meant optimum braking and roadholding from minimum metal. In the true style of Porsche, the 356 would take the philosophy a stage further.

There was scope for a bit more power, and the 1131cc engine's cylinder heads were modified (with slightly bigger valves and a compression ratio increased from 5.8:1 to 7.0:1) to give 35bhp compared to the standard 25; when a second downdraught carb was added, that went up to 40bhp. The clutch and non-syncromesh four-speed gearbox were used more or less as they came, in unit with the engine. Without any plan to give the Roadster more than two seats, the whole engine/gearbox assembly was turned through 180°, to give a mid-engined layout such as Porsche had long championed for racing, where compromises were rarely required.

That turned the rear suspension from trailing link to leading link, and put the transverse torsion bars right at the back of the chassis, which wasn't really desirable but short of a major redesign was unavoidable. The front suspension (also transverse torsion bars) was used without modification, and so were the cable-operated drum brakes and worm-and-roller steering, but instead of the VW's pressed-steel platform, the first 356 was designed around a tubular-steel chassis designed and fabricated in Gmünd, competition car-style.

The two-seater body had a competition connection too, although the car was always designed for a comfortable, roadgoing role. At least partly because sheet metal was hard to come by in 1948, the first 356 was designed as the simplest of open-topped Roadsters; what was left below the waistline,

The backward slope of the headlight units (above, left) mirrored that on the Beetle, and became a Porsche hallmark. Handmade body fittings such as the rearlight (top) show Porsche's talent for combining function with style. Trim (above) was minimal but designed for practicality.

The Roadster's dashboard (left) gave just enough information for a competition role, but a tachometer wasn't normally fitted to the first coupés — and the hadge wasn't designed until later. Body designer Komenda's quest for minimum aerodynamic drag shows in clever detailing such as the recessed and normally flush door handles (above).

356-1 ROADSTER SPECIFICATION

ENGINE
Flat-four, air-cooled

CAPACITY
1131cc

BORE x STROKE
75.0 x 64.0mm

COMPRESSION RATIO
6.5:1

POWER
35–40bhp

VALVE GEAR
Single central camshafts, pushrods

FUEL SYSTEM
Single Solex 26VFJ downdraught carburettor

TRANSMISSION
Four-speed manual

FRONT SUSPENSION
Independent, by trailing arms, transverse torsion bars, telescopic dampers

REAR SUSPENSION
Independent by swing axles, transverse torsion bars, lever-action dampers (reversed VW Beetle suspension

BRAKES
All drums, mechanically operated

WHEELS
Bolt-on, steel disc

WEIGHT
1289lb (585kg)

MAXIMUM SPEED
84mph (135kph)

NUMBER MADE, DATES
One (prototype), June 1948

though, clearly resembled a car that Porsche had designed for VW in 1939. That was the 60K10, to all intents and purposes a Beetle with a more powerful, 1.5-litre, flat-four engine and an ultra-streamlined, two-door coupé body, hand-formed in aluminium, with fully enclosed wheels. It was intended for an 800-mile road race to be run in September 1939 from Berlin to Rome (to celebrate the eponymous political Axis and show off the new autobahns and autostradas). Three cars were built, but the war started before the race was due to.

The 356 Roadster body was designed by Erwin Komenda and hand-formed in Gmünd by coachbuilder Friedrich Weber, who had known Porsche since the early 1920s at Austro-Daimler. It was made in aluminium and it didn't take much knowledge of aerodynamics to see that it was outstandingly smooth and slippery. On a wheelbase of 85 inches (2160mm) (9½ inches shorter than a Beetle's) it was very low and wide, but most of all it was very clean. The nose curved elegantly down (for good visibility as well as low drag), the wheels were well tucked in under softly sweeping wings; there was a low, steeply raked windscreen, and virtually no external trim save minimal bumpers and door handles. The headlamps raked back at the same angle as on the VW, and as they would later be on production 356s and on the 911; it is a strong Porsche styling note.

It was completed on 8 June 1948 and designated 356-1, and

it soon proved to be as effective as it was handsome. The whole car weighed barely 1300lb, or just 585kg, and even with only 40bhp that gave it very respectable acceleration for such a small engined car in its day. The lack of weight also helped it to achieve exceptionally short braking distances and fine roadholding – although the latter was not without problems, especially at the rear where the enforced re-orientation of the suspension gave the tubular chassis a hard time. The brilliance of the body shape was reflected in the fact that with so little power (and an open top) 356-1 could achieve not far short of 85mph, a figure which wouldn't disgrace many a late 1940s car with an engine of at least twice the Porsche's size. A month or so after it was completed, the very first Porsche scored the very first Porsche competition victory, with a class win in a race at Innsbruck, driven, appropriately enough, by Ferry Porsche's cousin Herbert Kaes.

So, all in all, 356-1 was considered to be a resounding success, but it was only one car and by the time it was completed the next 356s were already well under way. There would be two new body styles, a coupé and a cabriolet, and they would be rather different under the skin as well, for practicality and ease of construction. With them (and with more than a little help from a rapidly expanding and enthusiastically supportive VW) Porsche began the leap from first prototype to true series production of the Porsche marque.

356
COUPÉ

With 356-1 on the road from June 1948, things were starting to happen quite quickly at Gmünd, especially considering the almost backyard size of Porsche's operation in the former sawmill, the parlous state of supplies as local industries fought their way to post-war recovery, and the sheer weight of bureaucracy implicit in every acquisition and sale. Initially, Porsche survived pretty much on a day-to-day basis, scrounging and scavenging parts and materials wherever they could, but in the long term, once again, VW would be the key to Porsche progress.

On the strength of 356-1, they had found some financial support from two Swiss businessmen, Herr Senger and Herr Blank, whose interests included an advertising agency based in Zurich. With their help, Porsche gained limited access to VW parts, from the VW agency which had been set up in Switzerland as early as 1945. Switzerland could also supply sheet aluminium, but the Austrian authorities would only

sanction its import if Porsche agreed to export whatever cars they produced, to earn much needed foreign currency. Thus, 356-1 was sold, via Herr Senger, in Switzerland, together with the first four 'production' cars, which were all coupés and very different under the skin from the prototype Roadster, while still retaining the type number 356.

The changes showed that Porsche were serious about building in quantity rather than just as one-offs. The welded tubular frame of 356-1 had served its purpose in speeding the first car into existence, but Porsche knew from the start that such a construction method would be too time-consuming and expensive for even limited series production, and it was also rather bulky.

Even more fundamentally, Porsche acknowledged that a production model had to be more practical and comfortable, especially in terms of providing some luggage space (of which 356-1 had virtually none) and better isolating the passengers

The cockpit of the early 356 coupé, such as this 1951 example (left), was more hospitable than the spartan interior of 356-1. The first body style, with the two-piece windscreen (overleaf), survived until 1952. When production moved from Gmünd to Stuttgart the two 'screen panels were made slightly curved rather than flat.

It's unlikely that the racing style mirror (below) was an original fitting on this car, and virtually all that could fit under that front hatch in the early days was the spare wheel, fuel tank and a windscreen washer bottle.

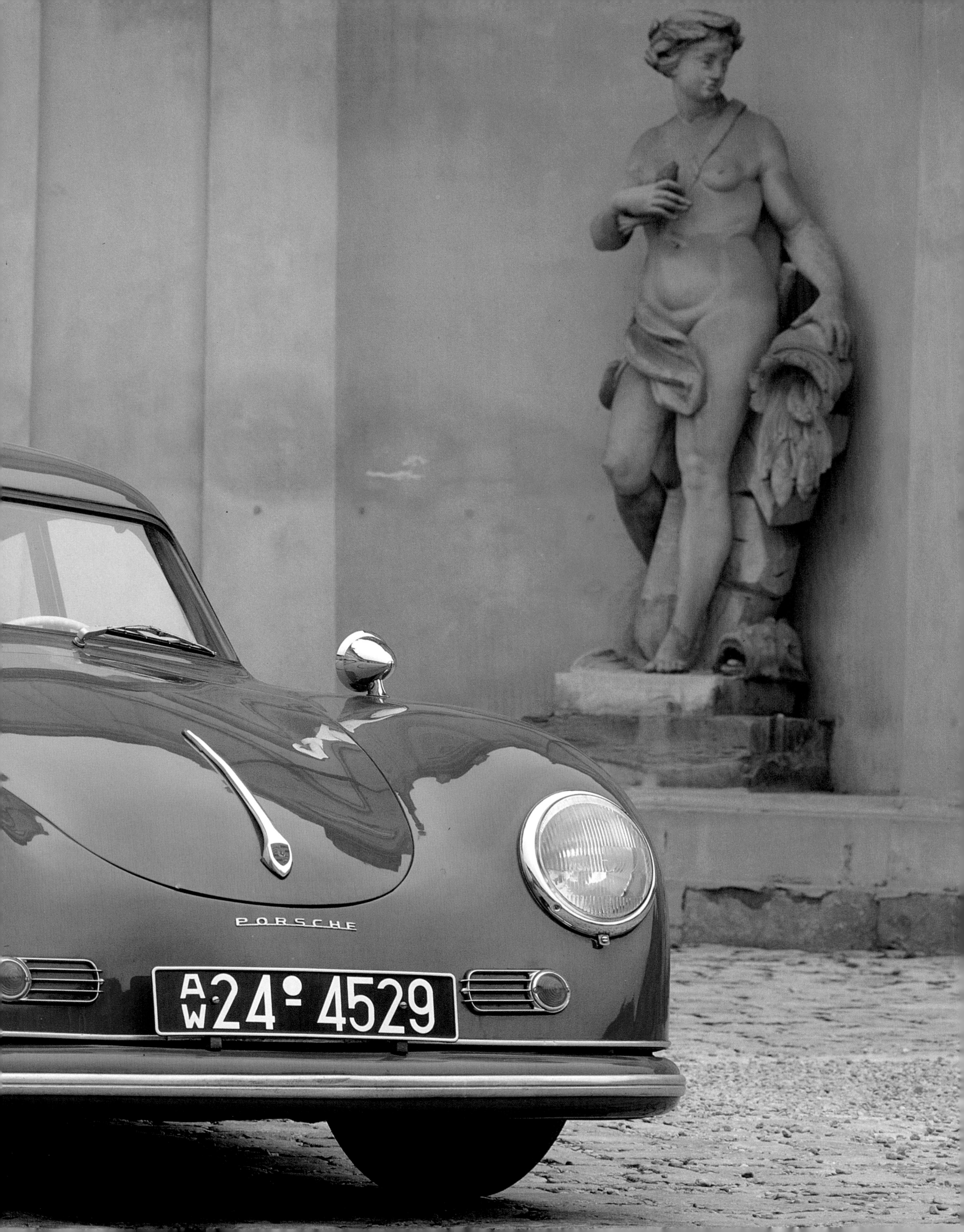
PORSCHE
AW 24 - 4529

from engine noise, heat and vibration, not to mention the weather.

Furthermore, turning the engine and gearbox around to give the mid-engined layout had involved more modification than Porsche strictly wanted to make in the transmission, and reversing the rear suspension had introduced problems of its own, in handling to some extent, but more worryingly in reliable mounting of the transverse torsion bars, which were less happy right at the back of the chassis than in their original location between engine and cockpit. The obvious way of solving most of the problems at a stroke was to go back to the VW layout as designed, with the engine behind the rear wheels and the suspension trailing as intended. That would liberate some luggage space behind the seats and move the noise and vibration away from the passengers; and in that the engine weighed barely 170lb (77kg), it would do little to harm the handling once balanced out by putting such heavy items as the battery, fuel tank and spare wheel under the nose.

As for the chassis, Porsche reverted to a VW-like steel platform. It was shorter in the wheelbase, of course, and more robust, with deep box-section sills, a shallow but strong centre tunnel (through which the gear-linkage and other services could run) and fabricated box structures for the engine bay and footwells. Different as it was in detail, it was along the same, easy-to-build lines as the VW platform and it was light enough to be lifted by one man.

Erwin Komenda was again responsible for the bodywork, and his first coupé was very similar to the Roadster up to the waistline (save for a slightly different nose with more rounded bonnet opening), surmounted by quite a narrow cabin, sweeping smoothly into a fastback tail and engine cover. There was a split windscreen and separate front quarter lights, but the classic 356 coupé shape was already all but set. The tail was a little different, in having a slightly incongruous vertical panel, apparently for a number plate, and details like light fittings and louvres had a decidedly hand-crafted look on the earliest cars, but the build quality was excellent and all these early 356s were still bodied in aluminium. The fact that there were minor variations from car to car was mainly a reflection of Porsche's policy of improving through experience . . .

There were variations in mechanical detail too, in this case largely because Porsche had to use what parts they could get. As with 356-1, almost everything was pure VW, including the engine, clutch, gearbox, suspension and steering, but the coupé was some 250lb (113kg) heavier than the Roadster so Porsche had started to fit more powerful Lockheed drum brakes, imported from Britain. Some used the same 1131cc flat-four as on 356-1, but Porsche quickly standardised a slightly shorter stroke version, of 1086cc, which conveniently fell within the 1100cc racing category and which, with a bit more work around the cylinder heads, was still quoted as producing 40bhp at 4200rpm. The heavier coupé was perhaps a bit slower off the mark than the Roadster, but with even better aerodynamics it was capable of over 85mph in comfort.

In March 1949, Porsche took another step towards becoming an established marque when they made their first ever motor show appearance, in Geneva. And they must have done so with new optimism, because late in 1948 their future had

Nominally at least there was some 'occasional' space behind the 356's front seats (above), but the intrusion of the gearbox now that it lived in front of the engine clearly made the space more useful for luggage than other people. Details such as lights and bumpers (left) changed from time to time, but the logo style was fixed by now.

The flat-four air-cooled
engine, while unashamedly
Beetle-derived, soon started
to become more Porsche and
less V W, a shorter stroke
giving 1086cc for most cars –
to qualify for 1100cc racing
classes. A 1300cc engine, with
10 per cent more power (or
44bhp!) was offered in 1951.

**356 COUPÉ
SPECIFICATION**

ENGINE
Flat-four, air-cooled

CAPACITY
1086cc

BORE x STROKE
73.5 × 64.0mm

COMPRESSION RATIO
7.0:1

POWER
40bhp

VALVE GEAR
Single central camshaft, pushrods

FUEL SYSTEM
Two downdraught Solex
32PBIC carburettors

TRANSMISSION
Four-speed manual

FRONT SUSPENSION
Independent, by trailing arms,
transverse torsion bars,
telescopic dampers

REAR SUSPENSION
Independent, by swing axles,
transverse torsion bars,
telescopic dampers

BRAKES
All drums; originally mechanical
operation, all later cars have
hydraulic operation

WHEELS
Bolt-on, steel disc

WEIGHT
c.1642lb (745kg)

MAXIMUM SPEED
87mph (140kph)

NUMBER MADE, DATES
4670, 1100 coupés, 1950–54

become a lot more secure. On 1 January 1948, control of V W had passed to former Opel executive Heinrich Nordhoff, who would run the company with outstanding flair until ill-health forced him to step aside in the early 1970s. Ferry Porsche had met Nordhoff during the war, and where V W's military caretaker management had been reluctant to enter into outside arrangements, Nordhoff was more than happy to establish a formal agreement with Porsche.

Thus, from mid-September 1948, Porsche became official design consultants to V W, received a DM5 royalty on each Beetle sold, and became Austrian agents for V W. Best of all perhaps, they were assured of a supply of parts for their own sports cars, and came to an agreement whereby they could sell the cars through the V W dealer network and have them serviced by V W agents.

This, of course, put a whole different complexion on Porsche production, and it became clear that the operation as it stood in Gmünd would soon be totally inadequate. The most desirable move would obviously be back to the old works in Stuttgart, and Porsche started negotiations to retrieve them from the Americans who were still leasing them, but in the event that didn't materialise until 1955. In the meantime, Porsche came to an arrangement with body-builders Reutter,

whose works were also in Stuttgart, and in November 1949 placed an order for 500 356 shells, with a reciprocal arrangement that Porsche should take over some space in the works for the mechanical assembly. In that the total production at Gmünd from June 1948 to March 1951 would be forty-six cars (including a handful of cabriolets designed by Swiss coach-builder Beutler), it was an ambitious move, but with the new agreement with V W, Porsche could afford it.

In going into true series production, the 356 changed again, in one major way and several small ones. The big change was from aluminium to steel for the bodies; smaller ones included more wrap-around for the halves of the split windscreen, which removed the need for the front quarter-lights. The brakes were changed too, to a V W hydraulic system, but otherwise, when the first German-built 356 was completed during Easter 1950, it was little different from its Austrian-built cousins.

True to Porsche philosophy, it didn't stay unchanged for long. At the Frankfurt Show in April 1951 there was a 44bhp, 1300cc engine option, and at the Paris Salon six months later a 1500. Porsche's original notion that they might produce a total of 500 cars had evaporated; they had already built more than twice that.

356
LIGHTWEIGHT
COUPÉ

As Porsche were starting series production of the steel-bodied 356 coupé in Stuttgart, they were also taking full advantage of the lightweight, aluminium-bodied Gmünd cars to make their first serious forays into international motor sport. Before that, from the late 1940s, Porsche customers had campaigned their own cars, and started winning in everything from road races to rallies, but this was different; now it was the factory's turn. With Porsche's background, that had only been a matter of time; with their expertise, winning could only be a matter of time, too.

As with all else, Porsche approached motor sport in a thoroughly methodical way. When it first seemed they might achieve some success, they estimated how much they might spend, weighed that against what they might spend on conventional advertising, compared the potential benefits, and decided that they really had to go racing. Of course, there may well have been other elements involved, like racing offering the opportunity for technical development, or even the simple fact that Porsche people *loved* racing, but the decision was taken with due logic.

So was the decision to use the earlier Gmünd cars for the first official racing efforts, simply because they were lighter than the new steel-bodied Stuttgart cars, and with their slightly narrower cabins they were just a valuable bit more aerodynamic.

That would be especially important for the race where Porsche chose to make their works racing debut, Le Mans, where everything was dominated by maximum speed on the long Mulsanne Straight, and where light weight was a pre-requisite for cars in the smaller classes; everything in the Porsche philosophy fitted the event.

Their French importer, one Auguste Veuillet, had recognised that and was ready to suggest some sort of involvement, but the real catalyst was Charles Faroux, veteran French motoring journalist and the man who, as editor of *La Vie Automobile* in the early 1920s, had conceived the race itself. Faroux was a firm friend of Professor Porsche. During Porsche's internment in France he had visited him regularly and when the time came it was Faroux who was the go-between who helped arrange his release. In October 1950 he

Even without the racing numbers on the doors, the shape of the lightweight coupé (right and overleaf) would leave little doubt as to its mission in life, with the covered wheel arches clearly aimed at optimum aerodynamics. The flat half-screens and curved windows are the proof that the car started from a Gmünd-built model.

Although it still had the VW flat-four (left) as its starting point, the first Porsche 'production' racer contrived a good deal more power than the standard item, with new camshafts, further improved cylinder heads, and improved carburation. They were tuned for reliability as much as for outright power.

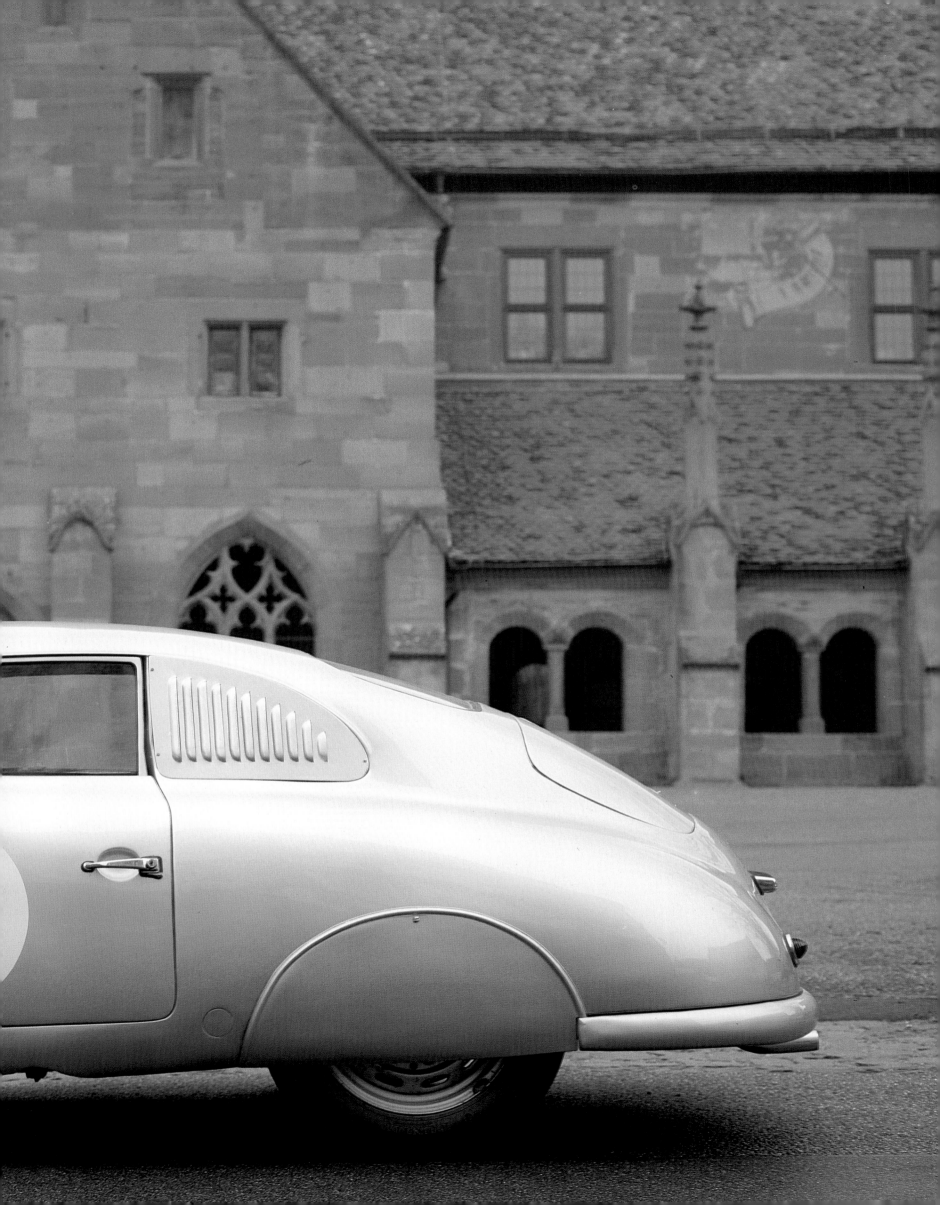

went to see the professor in Stuttgart, and it was then that he suggested Porsche might enter the great race in 1951.

A few months later, in March 1951, Auguste Veuillet, the enthusiastic French distributor, took his own 356 coupé to the Montlhéry track near Paris and proceeded to demonstrate to invited journalists that it would lap at more than 90mph (144kph). Shortly after, Faroux officially invited Porsche to race at Le Mans, and after due consideration they accepted.

They intended to send three of the Gmünd coupés, tuned to give significantly more power but not so much as to compromise reliability. The cars were to use the familiar 1086cc engines, to qualify them for the 1100cc class, but with further cylinder head work and new camshafts they were tuned to give slightly less than their theoretical peak, at some 46bhp, even on the notoriously poor and inconsistent French petrol. The lightweight coupé weighed approximately 1410lb (640kg) compared to about 1650lb for an early steel-bodied Stuttgart car, so the power to weight ratio was quite respectable at some 73bhp per litre, and there would be further bodywork refinements to give even lower drag – including fully-enclosed wheel arches and smooth panels below both nose and tail. Maximum speed was improved to just over 100mph (160kph).

For Le Mans, fuel tank capacity was increased to 78 litres (just over 17 gallons) by extending the tank forward and around the spare wheel, and a quick-fill fuel filler was added just ahead of the windscreen, in the middle of the strapped-down bonnet. The suspension used the usual torsion bars and there were drum brakes all round; a couple of extra driving

lights were added in the nose, and the sleek looking car was ready to go.

As well as the mechanical preparations, Porsche showed early signs of their later organisational skills in the way they planned their effort. To run the team, Ferry Porsche recruited Paul von Guilleaume, a German driver who had raced at Le Mans before the war, and preparation was done at the works. All did not go well, however, and Porsche lost three cars in various pre-race accidents. Even after juggling parts from the series of wrecks, that left them with only one raceable coupé – which was in fact the tenth of the first series cars built at Gmünd.

They made the most of the circumstances and entrusted the single entry (which carried race number 46) to Veuillet himself and fellow countryman Edmond Mouche, both of whom had raced at Le Mans before. They finished twentieth overall at an average speed of 73.6mph (118kph) and with a fastest lap of 87mph (140mph). They won the 1100cc class with some ease – at an average slightly *faster* than that for the winner of the 1500cc class. The same pair would return to Le Mans the following year to repeat their 1100 class win, and with the exceptions of 1959 (when, in a rare total failure, not a single Porsche finished) and 1965, Porsches were among the Le Mans class winners every year until they started their record run of outright wins in 1970.

After that 1951 Le Mans debut, the lightweight coupés gained more glory. In August, von Guilleaume and Count Heinz von der Muhle used one of the cars fitted with a new (and at that stage still secret) 1488cc engine, to win their class

The nose of this coupé, with the small grille, strapped down bonnet and twin driving lights (above and above left) is almost identical to the form in which the model first appeared (bearing the same number 46) at Le Mans in 1951. The big filler in the centre of the bonnet (top left) fed the additional tank capacity under the bonnet (also above) for long distance events.

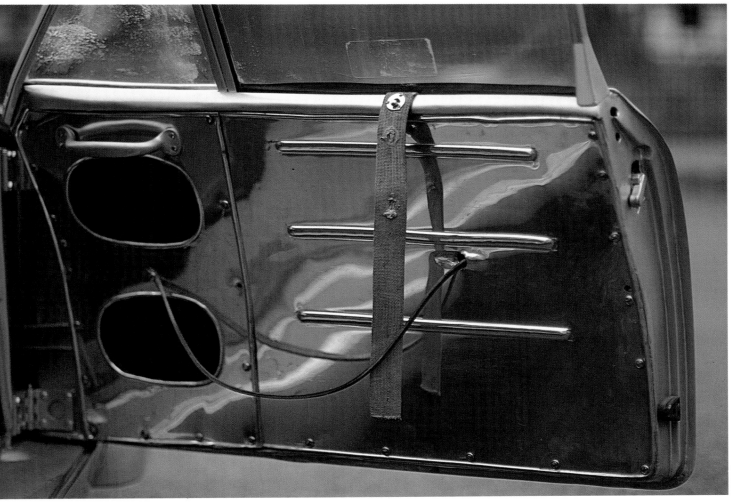

Lightness not luxury was the aim of the aluminium-bodied racing coupés, and details like the simple strap-operated side windows (left) saved precious pounds weight. The louvred rear side windows (left, below) helped cool both the engine and the cockpit.

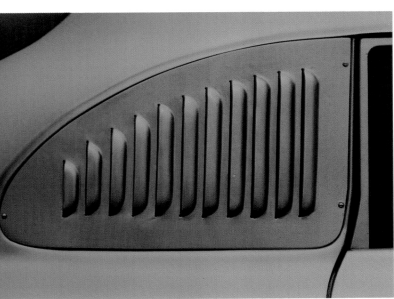

356 LIGHTWEIGHT COUPÉ SPECIFICATION

ENGINE
Flat-four, air-cooled

CAPACITY
1488cc (smaller capacity cars also built)

BORE x STROKE
80.0 x 74.0mm

COMPRESSION RATIO
8.2:1

POWER
70bhp

VALVE GEAR
Single central camshafts, pushrods

FUEL SYSTEM
Two downdraught Solex 32PBI carburettors

TRANSMISSION
Four-speed manual

FRONT SUSPENSION
Independent, by trailing arms, transverse torsion bars, telescopic dampers

REAR SUSPENSION
Independent, by swing axles, transverse torsion bars, lever-type dampers

BRAKES
All drums

WHEELS
Bolt-on, steel disc

WEIGHT
1410lb (640kg)

MAXIMUM SPEED
101mph (162kph)

NUMBER MADE, DATES
Five cars converted from Gmünd coupés, 1951

average of 95.2mph (153kph) (a distance of over 6850 miles), which was a world record for a 1½-litre car.

And remembering the equation between competition expenditure and advertising expenditure, Porsche promptly took the coupé to the Paris Salon, sat it on their stand and announced that a 60bhp version of the 1500 engine would henceforth be available as an option in the production 356.

Porsche then continued to compete with the lightweight coupés until well into the mid-1950s, latterly updating the shape with such production 356 details as one-piece windscreens, and proving successful in numerous events, notably the more punishing rallies and long-distance races. Among the successes listed against the lightweight coupé's name are class wins in the 1952 Coppa Inter-Europa at Monza, the 1953 Sestriere Rally, in the GP of Belgrade and the Rallye des Alpes in the same year, in the Luttich–Rome–Luttich rally of 1954, and the Zell am See ice races as late as 1955. Perhaps the biggest win for the lightweight coupés, though, came in 1952, in what was virtually a long distance race on open roads, the Liège–Rome–Liège Rally. The course covered over 3200 miles in under 90 hours, taking in 33 Alpine passes. Of the 106 entries, only 24 survived – including the entire Porsche team – and they were led home by a privately entered lightweight coupé driven by Helmut Polensky and Walter Schlüter. In 1954, a lightweight coupé won the event again, driven this time by Polensky and Herbert Linge. It used a new experimental engine, the first four-cam 1.5-litre flat-four destined to be used in everything from the Carrera to F2. The decision to go racing was fully justifying itself at Porsche.

in another, very different endurance event, the Liège–Sofia–Liège Rally – also taking a remarkable third place overall in what was considered one of the toughest tests of all. An 1100-engined lightweight, driven by Baron Huschke von Hanstein and Petermax Muller, finished second in its class.

In October, two of the Gmünd coupés were back at Montlhéry and attacking records. One had the normal 1086cc engine, the other was fitted with the new 1488cc engine, in this case giving as much as 72bhp. Both cars contributed to an impressive list of short- and long-distance records. The 1100 set marks from 500 miles to six hours, at up to 101.4mph (163kph); and the bigger car circulated for 72 hours at an

356A
1600S COUPÉ

On 16 March 1956, Porsche celebrated the 25th anniversary of the founding of Dr. Ing. h.c. F. Porsche GmbH, and during the large party they presented their 10,000th production car, driven off the production line by Ferry Porsche's youngest son, Wolfgang. It was a 356A coupé, and it showed just how far both the company and the 356 model had progressed since the first cars had been hand-built in Gmünd, just eight years before.

The very fact that there *was* a 10,000th 356 must in itself have been a source of considerable satisfaction – or possibly even amazement. When they started building the 356 in series, in 1950, Porsche more or less expected the total run to be no more than 500 examples, and their initial capital of DM 200,000 exactly covered the first order of 500 steel shells from Reutter, as commissioned in November 1949.

It wasn't necessarily such a dramatic underestimate as it seems with hindsight. So soon after the war, Europe had more urgent purchasing priorities than new sports cars, and maybe especially German ones, but the situation changed with remarkable speed.

Early in 1950, Porsche took two 356s, a coupé and a Beutler cabriolet, to a meeting of VW dealers in Wolfsburg, and they came away with thirty-seven orders – all for Europe, but almost half of them from outside of Germany. The deposits apparently came to almost precisely DM200,000, which was a convenient coincidence. Then in October 1950, Professor Porsche went to the Paris Show, where he met one Maximillian Hoffman of New York, and thereafter Porsche's horizons expanded dramatically.

Max Hoffman was an American citizen but of Austrian descent, and he was a sports car fanatic. Part of his vision was to get German cars back onto the US market, and Porsches were just his kind of car. So the man who would later be instrumental in the creation of the Mercedes 300SL 'gullwing' as a production car came to one of his first import arrangements with Porsche, and the long, happy relationship threw Porsche's market wide open.

On 21 March 1951, Porsche passed the notional 500 total; on 28 August of the same year the 1000th 356 was built; by 15 March 1954 they were up to number 5000; and number 10,000 was there for the celebrations of March 1956. America had been the key, of course, and Porsche had taken it by storm. With the benefit of Hoffman's flamboyant and expert promotion, almost universal rave notices from the specialist press,

By 1956, the 356's lines had developed subtly with the 356A, which now had a curved one-piece windscreen and a newly padded dashboard (far left). The wheel size had been reduced from 16-inch diameter to 15-inch, which gave a squatter, more modern look, and chrome plated steel wheels with centre lock hubs were an attractive option (overleaf).

The twin round tail-lights (left) only survived on the 356A through the 1956 model year and the early part of 1957, after which they were replaced by single teardrop-shaped lenses – the number plate light being moved at the same time, from above to below the plate.

and a rapidly growing list of competition successes, a Porsche was coming to be the car for *the* sporty driver in the early 1950s. Very quickly indeed, more than 50 per cent of 356 production found itself bound for the USA, and by the late 1950s the total proportion of Porsches exported from Germany was some 70 per cent.

That did give the Americans in particular some considerable say in what they wanted of the cars, but given that what the knowledgeable and unfailingly enthusiastic Hoffman ordered was almost invariably in line with Porsche's policy of constant improvement, that was no bad thing. So the 356, while keeping its essential character, gradually evolved.

The keynotes were obvious ones: more power for more performance; more flexibility for more relaxing road manners; better brakes to help exploit the improving performance; and steadily developing suspension, both for better handling and more comfort. The VW parts bin days had been very short-lived, and the flat-four engine had become more and more completely Porsche, almost from day one. New alloy cylinder heads with inclined exhaust valves had been designed by 1951, and a change from the original steel-lined barrels to wholly alloy barrels with a hard chrome-plated bore had saved around 2lb weight for each cylinder and at the same time offered the chance of taking the capacity from the original 1086cc to 1286cc, via bigger bores.

By late 1952, Porsche offered the 1100 and 1300 options, plus a new 1500, which had involved lengthening the stroke for the first and last time in the original VW-style block. In fact the 1488cc engine had first been contrived around a built-up, Hirth crankshaft with roller big-end bearings, but that was a very expensive way to build the engines, and Porsche also designed a new, forged, plain-bearing crankshaft to give the same capacity. Both versions were kept as options; the Hirth type gave a bit more power in the 'Super' engines, but it was less refined, less flexible and needed considerably more maintenance; the plain bearing crank was a great deal cheaper, smoother running and very long lived, at the expense of ultimate power and torque; and, of course, it was much the most common choice.

Through these variants, power had gone from the 40bhp of the original 1100 to 44bhp for the 1300, 55 for the normal 1500 and up to 60bhp for the 1500 Super, always with a bit more available for racing. The 74mm stroke of the 1488cc engine, however, was the most that the original block architecture would stretch to, because of the closeness of crankshaft and central camshaft, and when the 1600 pushrod engine (as distinct from the short-stroke, four-cam 1600 Carrera type) was introduced, in 1955, it had been further revised to allow a slightly bigger bore again, for a capacity of 1582cc. As with the 1500 engines, Porsche offered both ordinary and Super versions, the latter with the Hirth-type roller crankshaft, with the same implications of cost and power versus refinement and longevity.

The basic 1600 now gave 70bhp at 4500rpm and 82lb ft of torque at 2700rpm, the Super gave 88bhp at 5000rpm and 86lb ft of torque at a markedly less flexible 3700.

Of course, all the power increases had been matched by chassis modifications, for comfort and safety as well as for

The 1600 Super badge (above) represented the top spec of 356A, with 88bhp from its roller crankshaft engine. By this time, Porsche had also added the familiar 'heraldic' crest to their badging (left) featuring the black prancing horse of the city of Stuttgart.

The prancing horse was also evident in coachbuilder Reutter's badge (left), the Stuttgart company which had been given the contract to build the first 500 356 shells in November 1949 going on to build the cars in their tens of thousands.

As well as growing more powerful, the 356 was also becoming steadily more practical, with such niceties on this 356A as fully reclining front seats and folding rear seat backs (left) to give more versatile accommodation. The new dashboard (below left) had speedometer, rev-counter and combined fuel-level and oil-temperature gauges.

improved performance. Twin-leading-shoe front brakes with bigger, finned drums had been specified as early as 1951, and at the Paris Show in 1952 Porsche had publicly announced their newly patented syncromesh system – a brilliant design which improved the now all-syncro 356 gearbox enormously and also earned Porsche huge amounts of money in licence fees, as it was adopted by numerous major manufacturers for many years to come.

The windscreen had gone from two-piece to one-piece in 1952, a rev counter, fuel gauge and clock had been added to the original speedo-only dash layout, while reclining front seats, folding rear seat backs and better soundproofing all improved comfort from around 1953.

By the 1956 model year, there were more changes: the windscreen had a more pronounced wrap around (known at the time as the 'panorama look'), the wheels had been changed to a smaller but wider and more modern 15-inch diameter type (with the option of chromed rims and centre-lock fixing), and the suspension had been refined too, with slightly softer torsion bars and longer travel, plus a front anti-roll bar and better dampers. The starting point for that was obviously an American desire for a more comfortable car, but in fact it suited the 356 very well, and far from turning it into a soft and sloppy boulevard cruiser it made it a more supple and predict-able car in most conditions. Then, of course, there was the option of the new 1600 engines, a further improved gearbox, a much tidier dashboard and plenty of other smaller detail refinements.

It was clearly a very different car from the 356 of only a few years earlier and Porsche acknowledged the fact by changing the designation to 356A for the 1956 model year, and there were other signs of progress too, in that the car was now available in three distinct body styles – coupé, cabriolet and Speedster, the last of which was another Hoffman suggestion and one of the most memorable Porsches of all. . .

356A 1600S COUPÉ SPECIFICATION

ENGINE
Flat-four, air-cooled

CAPACITY
1582cc

BORE x STROKE
82.5 x 74.0mm

COMPRESSION RATIO
8.5:1

POWER
75bhp

VALVE GEAR
Single central camshaft, pushrods

FUEL SYSTEM
Two downdraught solex 40PBIC carburettors

TRANSMISSION
Four-speed manual

FRONT SUSPENSION
Independent, by trailing arms, transverse torsion bars, telescopic dampers, anti-roll bar

REAR SUSPENSION
Independent, by swing axles, transverse torsion bars, telescopic dampers

BRAKES
All drums

WHEELS
Bolt-on, steel disc (centre-lock optional)

WEIGHT
1940lb (880kg)

MAXIMUM SPEED
112mph (180kph)

NUMBER MADE, DATES
5981 (incl. all body styles), 1956–9

356A 1600 SPEEDSTER

Max Hoffman really loved Porsches, and Porsche could only have loved Max, for his unflagging efforts to open up the American market. His dealership, on Park Avenue, New York, became almost single-handedly responsible for re-opening the American market to European cars after World War II, and especially to European sports cars. Within a few years, Max was selling VWs and Mercedes, BMWs and, of course, Porsches. And with his Austrian ancestry, he was genuinely a friend of the family.

When Hoffman met Professor Ferdinand Porsche at the Paris Show in October 1950, and arranged to import the first Porsches into America, Porsche, ailing ever since his release from internment after the war, didn't have very long to live. In November, the 75-year-old Porsche visited the VW factory and was deeply moved by the scale and success of the operation he had set in motion, but shortly after he returned home, he suffered a stroke and his health started its final decline. He remained bed-ridden, if apparently as stubborn and as mentally active as ever, but on 30 January 1951 he died. His son Ferry, of course, was already in actual control of the Porsche companies, and so the dynasty continued, and so did the relationship with Max in America.

In 1952 it was Hoffman who set up contracts between Porsche and Studebaker, the outcome of which was supposed to be that Porsche would act as consultants to Studebaker and design a new, sporty car for them, probably with an air-cooled rear-mounted six-cylinder engine, and aerodynamic lines. The contacts went on for some time, and prototypes were even built, but in the end the project was stillborn, partly because Studebaker had an attack of conservatism when they saw Porsche's early proposals, partly because they lacked the technical resources to build anything quite so advanced, but mostly because they were in dire financial straits and about to be absorbed by Packard.

It was Hoffman who looked after Ferry Porsche while he was on this second post-war visit to America, and it was Hoffman who, during this visit, urged Porsche to come up with a proper badge. Sitting with Max in a New York restaurant, Ferry sketched a 'coat of arms' on the back of a napkin, which he eventually gave to Komenda back in Stuttgart to tidy up into a usable design. It used the crest of the House of Württemberg and the prancing black horse of the city of Stuttgart, all surmounted by the Porsche name; within a year Ferry Porsche's design had become the official Porsche

The Speedster's distinctive 'inverted bathtub' lines (right and overleaf) probably weren't the sort of thing that Porsche would ever have drawn themselves, but they trusted Max Hoffman's knowledge of the US market implicitly, and Max was soon given his chopped-down 356 hot-rod.

The Speedster was designed to offer more for less, with trim and equipment reduced to basics to save both weight and cost; but what he had taken away in savings Hoffman piled back on with flamboyant style, as in the swoopy mirrors (below).

badge and it has been on every Porsche car since.

Max also looked after the Porsche racing team during their first forays into America and during one such trip he had arranged a party to introduce the Porsche people to the press, and gain appropriate publicity. Come party time, however, and Porsche's star driver, Karl Kling (on loan from Mercedes), was still inexplicably detained by the immigration authorities on Ellis Island; and in spite of the best efforts of the German embassy he stayed there until the party was almost over. In the meantime, Porsche racing manager Baron Huschke von Hanstein had stood in at the party, and the talk had been of racing and of sports cars.

And when Max Hoffman talked sports cars, even the biggest manufacturers listened, because Max clearly knew what Americans would buy, and he could back his judgement with *big* orders. In 1953 he suggested to Mercedes that they might like to turn their new 300SL racing car into a production car, but Mercedes weren't convinced. Max promised 1000 firm orders, the car appeared at the New York Show in January 1954, and the Gullwing was born.

Now, also in 1954, he had an idea for a new version of the 356, which he knew would be just the thing for his younger and more flamboyant American customers. The secret would be that he would delete anything the car didn't actually need, which would bring down both the weight and the price; he would give it a distinctive look, and he would sell it as a sporty special edition at a rock-bottom price. He would call it the Speedster.

Porsche were happy to oblige, even though the Speedster was originally only envisaged as a US market model, and the car was soon in Max's showrooms. Reutter built it, and up to the waist it was basically identical to any 356 cabriolet, but then the windscreen was some 3½ inches (88mm) lower, steeply raked and very curvaceous, and set in a slim chrome frame rather than in the body coloured moulding of the cabrio. A chrome strip running the full length of the flanks, through door-handle height, further emphasised the lowness. The top was as truncated as the 'screen, and very rudimentary, providing little headroom and even less real protection from wind and rain. The wind-up door windows had been deleted, in favour of lightweight plastic sidescreens, there were special bucket seats and a minimalist dashboard design with passenger grab-handle, but not much else.

It was a lot lighter than the more elaborately equipped cabrio and had slightly lower gearing, to emphasise the acceleration even more. In May 1955, Hoffman–Porsche Cars Corpn were able to advertise it for the extremely attractive price of just $2995, delivered in New York and with 'all extras' included. In reality it wasn't much more than a cabrio built to minimum spec and bargain basement price, but Max had given it *style* and nobody would ever feel inferior in a Speedster.

Initially it offered a choice of 1500 or 1500S power, which meant 55 or 70bhp, and that was good enough for a claimed maximum of 100mph (160kph), plus superior acceleration thanks to the lower weight and gearing, and better roadholding thanks to a significantly lower centre of gravity. A little later, as the Carrera Speedster, it added the option of a 100 or, finally, 110bhp version of the four-cam, short-stroke, 1500 race-type engine, as used for the Spyder and the new Carrera

Even the 'wind-swept' Speedster graphics and the full-length chrome trim-strip running through the line of the door handles (above and right) were contrived to give the car a longer and lower look – but for minimal outlay, of course.

In open-topped form – either Speedster or cabriolet – the 356 needed some reshaping around the tail (left) to provide the clearance for the engine cooling fan that the coupé's fastback line accommodated more naturally. Bucket seats and minimal trim distinguish the cockpit.

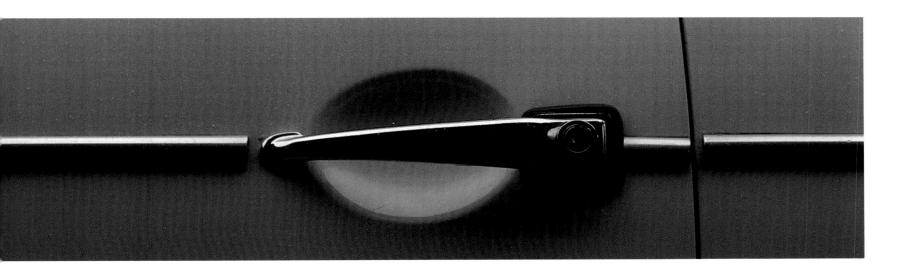

coupés. With that engine, it was even more rapid and not surprisingly it carved itself quite a useful racing career. The ultimate version was offered in 1957, as the GT Carrera Speedster, with an engine virtually to Spyder spec, Spyder front brakes, Spyder steering, adjustable dampers, alloy doors, boot and bonnet lids, lighter seats and even less trim – which in spite of built-in roll bar mounts and a bigger fuel tank saved around another 140lb (63kg). It was very quick.

It was also the Speedster's swansong. From being a US-only model, the cars had been offered in Europe, and sold pretty well everywhere; and when the 356A appeared with the new 1600 and 1600S engines, the Speedster got them too, with 60 and 75bhp respectively; but it never graduated to a 1600 Carrera spec.

Instead, in 1958, the Speedster was reincarnated as the 356 Convertible D, in which the D stood for a new body-builder, Drauz of Heilbronn. The look was broadly similar, but

Hoffmann's very pure philosophy of minimum trim, maximum style, minimum price was being diluted – presumably for European tastes and the scope for better profit margins. The Convertible D had a slightly taller windscreen, a better hood (which wasn't difficult) and even wind up door windows. It was a lot more like a cabrio than the true Speedster, and the price reflected that. When the 356B line started, in 1960, the Convertible D in turn became the Roadster D – and survived as such until 1963, but few would argue that it had the sheer style of the original Speedster.

And finally, the Speedster name reappeared in 1989 on a version of the 911. It had a chopped down top and a certain ugly charm, but instead of stripping it bare and selling it for less, Porsche piled on a high-luxury specification, kept it as a strictly limited edition which brought in the speculators, and asked for a great deal more money. What would Max Hoffman have thought?

Even with the minimalist approach, the Speedster's painted-metal dash (below, left) looked good, and it offered all the information a sporty driver would ever need to know – including a rev-counter in the centre, a 120mph speedometer, and the familiar combined fuel-level and oil-temperature gauge.

356A 1600 SPEEDSTER SPECIFICATION

ENGINE
Flat-four, air-cooled

CAPACITY
1582cc

BORE x STROKE
82.5 x 74.0mm

COMPRESSION RATIO
7.5:1

POWER
60bhp

VALVE GEAR
Single central camshaft, pushrods

FUEL SYSTEM
Two downdraught Solex 32PBIC carburettors

TRANSMISSION
Four-speed manual

FRONT SUSPENSION
Independent, by trailing arms, transverse torsion bars, telescopic dampers, anti-roll bar

REAR SUSPENSION
Independent, by swing axle, transverse torsion bars, telescopic dampers

BRAKES
All drums

WHEELS
Bolt-on, steel disc (centre-lock optional)

WEIGHT
1840lb (835kg)

MAXIMUM SPEED
100mph (160kph)

NUMBER MADE, DATES
n/a (included in 356A total) 1956–9

356B SUPER 90 ROADSTER

A decade after the first Porsches had gone into something like series production, in Gmünd and then in Stuttgart, the 356 might at first glance have looked pretty much as it always did, but in reality it was a very different car indeed, and a much improved one. That was the Porsche way, and there was rarely a year in the history of the 356 when it didn't change for the better.

It started its continuous evolution virtually as soon as it came off the drawing board, not least with the switch from hand-made aluminium bodies to the series-built steel ones from Reutter, and with the adoption of the special, Porsche-built inclined-valve aluminium cylinder heads as early as 1949. The 1950 cars had hydraulic brakes, and for 1951 the Stuttgart-based piston manufacturer, Mahle, had developed the system of chrome plating and etching the bores of linerless aluminium cylinder barrels which allowed the four-cylinder engine to grow for the first time, to become a 1300.

Capacity went up again later in the same year, when Porsche used the expensive and complex built-up Hirth roller crankshaft to sidestep the problem of minimal crank to camshaft clearance, increase the stroke for the first time and arrive at the first 1500 engine. That put power up quite dramatically, eventually to as much as 70bhp for the 1500, but Porsche were just as diligent in developing the chassis and running gear of the 356 as they were in making it more powerful and quicker. Accordingly, the car also gained twin-leading-shoe front brakes, and telescopic dampers at the rear, in place of the more old-fashioned lever-arm type with which the car had been introduced – so it now went faster, cornered better and stopped harder.

For 1952 it changed cosmetically, but ever so subtly. The split windscreen was replaced by a one-piece type, though still with a definite vee-shape, and the bumpers were separated a little way from the body. The interior was made a bit more hospitable, with a tachometer, clock and fuel gauge joining the originally minimal instrumentation, plus reclining front seats and foldable rear seat backs – to give more versatility for carrying luggage or occasional, hardy passengers. A radio was offered as an option, the superb Porsche-patent all-syncromesh gearbox was available, and the 1500 engine was

The 356B Roadster with its chrome-framed windscreen had something of the character of the earlier generation Speedster in its lines (far left and overleaf) but with a good deal more refinement – and at a considerably higher price. The small grilles by the protruding side lights cover the horns and the ones below the bumper cool the brakes.

One of the most obvious visual changes on the 356B was the way that the bumpers had been raised (below), to offer better protection from minor bodywork damage. At the same time, the headlamps were also raised slightly, which gave a flatter line to the front wings.

offered in a plain-bearing variant, with 55bhp. The Hirth roller-bearing engine continued as the 1500S, for Super; and the plain-bearing 1500-engined cars were affectionately nicknamed *Damen*, or ladies, for their gentler and more refined demeanours.

The badge that Ferry Porsche had drawn over dinner in a New York restaurant with the irrepressible Max Hoffman had been tidied up by Komenda and now graced the nose of the cars, as it would in future generations.

1953 was a relatively quiet year in more ways than one in that there were very few real changes, but one of them was improved sound insulation for the cabin. The 1300 engine also became available in plain-bearing and roller-crank versions, the latter again suffixed S. The Speedster extended the range in 1954, but the long-serving 1100 engines were finally dropped, and Porsche moved further away from any but notional VW connections by adopting their own three-piece aluminium crankcases rather than the two-piece magnesium-alloy VW types used so far.

Late in 1955, Porsche announced the 356A for 1956, and, by their standards, that clearly meant that they had made even more changes than normal. Some of them were fairly small, like new door handles, standard windscreen washers, and moving the heater controls from the dash to the floor tunnel; some were cosmetic, like a more curved windscreen which finally lost the hint of a vee; and some of them were very fundamental, including a further improved transmission, and heavily revised suspension – which had softer torsion bars and longer travel, but also now a front anti-roll bar, all of which improved both ride *and* handling, taking at least some of the frequently remarked sting out of the tail.

Further contributing to that on these 1956 356A models was more modern footwear, with wider tyres on smaller diameter wheels, which also gave the car a decidedly more chunky look.

It had more power again, too, as Porsche managed to increase the bores of the 1500 engines again to create a family of 1600s, which were a bit more powerful and a lot more flexible, and helped with the continuing quest for gentility.

Unlike the other 356Bs, the Roadster made do without quarter-lights in the door windows (top left). The chassis plate appeared in the door pillar (bottom left), complete with engine specification details. The Roadster was considerably better trimmed and equipped inside (above) than the Speedster had ever been.

After another comparatively low-key year in 1957, marked only by minor styling updates including a change to neat, one-piece tail-lamp units, 1958 saw another minor avalanche of developments for the 356A as it neared the end of its first decade. In the never-ending pursuit of quieter and smoother running, Porsche dropped the 1600 roller-bearing engine in favour of a less highly strung (not to mention cheaper) plain-bearing type, and the original plain-bearing 1600 was given mainly cast-iron construction instead of its more expensive alloy casings, which made it a bit heavier but a lot quieter. A new steering box and a slightly bigger steering wheel reduced the steering effort which the wider tyres had brought, the clutch and gearchange were made a bit lighter to operate, and the exhaust tailpipes were re-routed through the bottoms of the rear bumper overriders; which gave better bump clearance and a tidier look, but blackened the tail fairly quickly.

And then at the Frankfurt Show, late in 1959, for the 1960 model year, the 356 reached what Porsche officially reckoned to be its third distinct incarnation, in the guise of the 356B.

By Porsche's standards, it looked dramatically different, with noticeably higher bumpers under which had appeared some cooling slots for the front brakes, and deeper glass all round to give a lighter look inside and out. There was more rear seat room, with split-folding seat backs, more luggage space under a reshaped nose, and further improved transmissions and suspension – the latter now incorporating a 'compensating' spring at the rear, which comprised a single transverse leaf running below the gearbox and with its ends picking up, via rubber bushes, on the trailing arms. The theory was that it allowed spring rates to be softer while stiffening the car in roll, which helped a lot with the famous lift-off and roll-oversteer characteristics. Radial tyres were offered as standard, too, for the first time on a 356.

A new engine was added to the 1600 and 1600S options, and dubbed the 1600 Super 90, which alluded to its power output, now a most impressive 90bhp at 5500rpm. It was a superb engine, usefully more lusty than the 75bhp 1600S but a lot more civilised than the rabid four-cam Carrera. It had bigger carbs, higher compression and a slightly wilder camshaft, but it matched its added power with more docility than any other example of the flat-four, and it was very popular.

And if you wanted the ultimate combination of performance with refinement and versatility, you could specify the Super 90 in Roadster form, the Roadster being the latest name in 356B nomenclature for what had started out as Max's Speedster in 1954, continued through the better-trimmed Convertible D from 1958, and had now come almost full circle to be a fully-trimmed, higher-rooflined, roll-up-windowed and far from cut-price model at the top rather than the bottom of the range. Even as a soft-top it was a comfortable 110mph (176kph) performer with sub-10-second 0–60mph abilities, and it was amongst the nicest of all the 356s.

There would be a 356C from 1964, but there weren't many more changes in between, because Porsche were busily engaged on something called the 901, which would soon replace the first generation. By then, well over 76,000 356s would have been built, and almost 31,000 of those were in the 356B family. At Porsche, practice makes perfect.

Teardrop rear lights and substantial over-riders on the raised bumpers (top left) help identify the 356B. The Super 90 engine (above) was a new option, combining most of the power of the four-cam Carrera unit with the civility of the lesser flat-fours. The fully trimmed hood (left) was a far cry from a Speedster's.

356B SUPER 90 ROADSTER SPECIFICATION

ENGINE
Flat-four, air-cooled

CAPACITY
1582cc

BORE x STROKE
82.5 x 74.0mm

COMPRESSION RATIO
9.0:1

POWER
90bhp

VALVE GEAR
Single central camshaft, pushrods

FUEL SYSTEM
Two twin-choke downdraught
Solex 40PII-4 carburettors

TRANSMISSION
Four-speed manual

FRONT SUSPENSION
Independent, by trailing arms, transverse torsion bars, telescopic dampers, anti-roll bar

REAR SUSPENSION
Independent, by swing axles, transverse torsion bars, telescopic dampers

BRAKES
All drums

WHEELS
Bolt-on, steel disc

WEIGHT
1995lb (905kg)

MAXIMUM SPEED
110mph (176kph)

NUMBER MADE, DATES
5694 (all body styles), 1960–63

356B
CARRERA GTL
ABARTH

Late in 1946, soon after Ferry Porsche had been allowed back to Austria from his brief internment, two old family friends arrived at the Porsche home in Zell am See. One was the engineer Rudolf Hruska, who had worked for Porsche before the war and had been closely involved with the VW project. The other was Carlo Abarth, a sometime motor-cycle racer who had moved back from his adopted Austria to his birthplace in Yugoslavia before the war started – helped by Ferry Porsche's brother-in-law Dr Anton Piëch, whose secretary had become Abarth's wife.

Now Hruska's and Abarth's paths had crossed and they were back in touch with their old friends. They had met in Merano in northern Italy, whence Abarth's family had originated and where he had gone to live immediately after the war. Early in 1945, Hruska had gone to Brescia to negotiate a parts manufacturing deal with commercial vehicle maker OM, but been unable to get back to Stuttgart because the Americans had moved in. He went to stay in Merano, and made contact with Abarth. By the time the Americans did allow them to visit Porsche in Austria, the two had decided that they would

like to represent the company in Italy, even though there was no actual product to sell!

Hruska and Abarth also had a commercial partner in Italy, one Piero Dusio, who was to play a major part in Porsche's immediate future. Dusio was a former champion athlete and football star whose career had been cut short by injury and who had gone on, before the war, to make a substantial fortune, first in the textile industry then in banking, hotels and sporting equipment, including bicycles. His sporting goods manufacturer was known as Consorzio Industriale Sportivo Italia – or Cisitalia.

Dusio was also an enthusiastic racing driver and sponsor, and during the war, with Fiat engineer Dante Giacosa, he had conceived a family of Fiat-powered single-seater and sports cars which could go into limited production as off-the-shelf racers. They were successful competitively and commercially, and Dusio also dabbled with road cars, but most of all he wanted a GP car.

In a nice piece of serendipity, Tazio Nuvolari, racing legend and one of the few men ever to master Prof. Porsche's pre-war

The Carrera GTL Abarth was substantially different in profile (overleaf) from the 356B on which it was based, sharing the same wheelbase but being a few inches longer overall than the standard car – notably in the extended nose (right) which normally carried additional driving lights alongside the air intake.

The Abarth (below) also had a decidedly more beetle-backed look than the standard Carrera, and with a lot more cooling vents cut into the lightweight aluminium shell. Variations in the shape of the side windows were largely a result of the shells being hand-built.

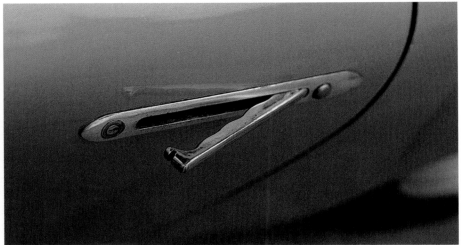

Auto-Union GP cars, was looking for a car with which to resume his career. A friend at OM put him in touch with Hruska in Merano; and, naturally, it was concluded that Porsche could design the GP car if someone could be found who would be willing enough to fund it.

Through mutual friends, Hruska and Abarth contacted Dusio (who already knew Nuvolari), and the pieces began to fall into place. An arrangement was reached between Dusio, Hruska, Abarth and Porsche where Porsche would design the GP car, a sports car and even a tractor for Dusio, who would pay all the fees. Dusio's payments were enough to pay the bond needed to expedite Professor Porsche's release from French internment, and initiate the start proper of Porsche's post-war growth.

The mid-engined, supercharged, four-wheel-drive GP car was a technical masterpiece, but the project collapsed when spiralling costs contributed to Cisitalia's bankruptcy. By early 1949, Dusio had sold the project to an equally unsuccessful Argentine company, but out of the ashes of Cisitalia, former chief mechanic Carlo Abarth emerged in April 1949 with his own company in Turin, and plans to build Abarth competition cars and tuning equipment for the wider market. His badge was a scorpion – his birth sign.

Over the next decade, Abarth built a considerable reputation as a racing car manufacturer, close links with Fiat, and a very healthy business manufacturing bolt-on tuning equipment. He also maintained loose but friendly contacts with Porsche, and in 1960 the two companies collaborated again, to build a spectacular, lightweight coupé – which meant that Porsche could campaign in the GT category of the World Championship for Makes.

It was the Porsche 356B Carrera GTL Abarth, and the starting point was the 356B Carrera, whose mechanical spec survived virtually intact under a new and very slippery all-aluminium body. Who drew and built that is a matter of some confusion, because the popular version says that Abarth designed the shell and Zagato (who would have been Porsche's first choice as stylist) built it, while some sources say it was built by (ex-Zagato man) Franco Scaglione, and some contend the shells were mostly built by an obscure Italian bodyshop in Turin by the name of Viarengo and Filliponi.

Whatever, Porsche were happy with the aerodynamic shape and the weight saving of more than 300lb over a steel-bodied Carrera, if apparently a little taken aback by the fairly rudimentary quality of Turin workmanship compared to the impeccable Stuttgart variety, which led them to do quite a lot of refinishing on the four or five cars which they retained for the works racing efforts.

The bodywork did look very different from the standard cars'. The wheelbase was the same, of course, but the Abarths

There wasn't much doubting that the Carrera Abarth was purely and simply a racing model, from the strapped-down bonnet (top left) to the aerodynamically recessed door handles (top right) and the single, central exhaust system (above), which was one of Carlo Abarth's commercial specialities.

The scorpion on Abarth's badge (above) was from Carlo Abarth's birth sign; the sting in the tail of the 356B Carrera GTL Abarth (left) ranged from the four-cam flat-four 1600 engine in standard 115bhp trim, to the 2-litre Carrera 2 engine, with up to 185bhp.

356B CARRERA GTL ABARTH SPECIFICATION

ENGINE
Flat-four, air-cooled

CAPACITY
1588cc

BORE x STROKE
87.5 x 66.0mm

COMPRESSION RATIO
9.8:1

POWER
135bhp

VALVE GEAR
Two overhead camshafts per cylinder bank

FUEL SYSTEM
Two twin-choke downdraught Weber carburettors

TRANSMISSION
Four-speed manual

FRONT SUSPENSION
Independent, by trailing arms, transverse torsion bars, telescopic dampers, anti-roll bar

REAR SUSPENSION
Independent, by swing axles, transverse torsion bars, telescopic dampers

BRAKES
All drums (some later converted to discs)

WHEELS
Bolt-on, steel disc

WEIGHT
1715lb (778kg)

MAXIMUM SPEED
137mph (220kph)

NUMBER MADE, DATES
20, 1960–62

were a few inches longer – notably in the nose, which was much less bluff. Barely two cars were the same, but the nose was always long and quite shark-like, sometimes with built-in driving lights flanking the slim air-intake, sometimes with perspex covers over the recessed headlights – but never with any bumpers, which had no place on this exclusively competition machine. At the back, the wings were a bit more distinct from the familiar beetle-back, and there were literally dozens of small louvres in the engine cover, plus a familiar Abarth trademark in the shape of a propped-open vent. Later cars had a detachable panel under the tail for easier engine access and removal. Hardly any two cars were completely identical in the shape of their side windows, but that was another characteristic of Italian hand-building.

Inside, the cars were trimmed as simply as possible, to the extent that most had pull-up rather than wind-up windows, and all windows except the windscreen were normally in lightweight Plexiglas.

Porsche supplied twenty-one chassis in 1960, but it seems that only eighteen were originally built up. The torsion-bar suspension with rear trailing arms was pure Carrera, and so were the finned drum brakes and the glorious four-cam, twin-plug flat-four engine – as derived from the original racing Carrera and now in production for over five years. The Abarth GTL *was* offered as a customer car, and every example

made was sold before it was built. At least four distinct stages of tune were offered. The first was the 1588cc engine in standard trim giving 115bhp; next was a 1588 with improved exhaust system (an Abarth speciality) and 128bhp; and then there was a 1588 with Solex rather than Weber carbs, and 135bhp. Later, the 1966cc Carrera 2 engine was offered, which gave anything from 155 to 185bhp and a top speed of over 140mph (225kph), which made the Abarth GTL comfortably the fastest of the 356 Carreras. Many early cars had the bigger engine fitted later, and some gained disc brakes to match.

Of course, Porsche had got their sums precisely right with the lightweight coupé, and for some three years it steamrollered its 2-litre class opposition in the GT ranks. It won its class first time out, in the 1960 Targa Florio (and finished sixth overall), and again in the Nürburgring 1000km, at Le Mans and at Sebring. In 1961 it scored points at Sebring, Le Mans, the Targa again and in the Paris 1000km; it completed the Targa hat-trick in 1962 and was seventh overall en route to another Sebring class win to add to another at the Nurburgring (where it was the first GT car ever to lap in under ten minutes). It won its GT championship class with considerable ease in 1961, 1962 and 1963, and even on its last major works outing, at Daytona as late as 1963, it managed fifth place overall. Not surprisingly, the Porsche with the Italian connection remains one of the most desirable of all.

718/8
RS SPYDER

In the Porsche Museum, at Stuttgart-Zuffenhausen, there is a car called 'Grandmother'. It is a 718/8 RS Spyder, chassis number 718 047, and it was given the affectionate nickname by the racing department mechanics who saw it on a regular basis during a competition life that was extraordinarily long and successful even by Porsche standards. In its simple silver paintwork it was campaigned all over the world, from Europe to America to the Bahamas and Puerto Rico, in circuit racing, long-distance road races and then with most success of all in the European Hillclimb Championships, between 1962 and 1964.

The 718/8 was the last of the classic first generation of Porsche competition Spyders, before the aluminium body construction was replaced by plastics in its successor the 904 GTS, and it was another fine example of Porsche developing a theme to its ultimate conclusion.

The open-topped competition cars marked a transition for Porsche into ever more serious racing commitment. They moved away from production-based models (amongst which you really had to number even the lightweight Gmünd

coupés) and on for the first time to cars built specifically for racing, recognising that motor sport was already becoming more specialised and more competitive. The first of the open topped factory racers appeared in 1953, when Porsche showed off the 550 at the Paris Salon, but it wasn't quite the first of the two-seater competition spyders.

Porsche were prompted to build their own after seeing the Porsche-engined specials built by Frankfurt distributor Walter Glöckler. Glöckler, with one of the factory engineers, had tuned an 1100 engine to give up to 58bhp, turned it round and mounted it ahead of the rear axle, in a tubular frame clothed in a very light, all-aluminium open body. Glöckler won the German sports car championship in 1950, his cars with other drivers won in 1951 and 1952; and his spyder, by now with a 90bhp 1500 engine, set numerous records alongside the factory coupés at Montlhéry in 1951, which clearly pointed the way for a works copy.

So the 550 was largely drawn up by works engineer Wilhelm Hild, initially using the new 1500 pushrod engine, tuned to give close to 100bhp on alcohol fuel. It used a fairly

'Grandmother' (left) was one of the last of the 'first generation' Porsche racing Spyders – the first cars that Porsche had built from the drawing board purely as racing models. This final series was the most aerodynamic to date, but the tubular spaceframe chassis was still bodied in aluminium (overleaf), where the next racing models would be clothed in plastics.

The superbly neat detailing around the nose of the 718 Spyder (left) was a typical example of the way Porsche could combine science with style; the headlamps are smoothly faired in behind long perspex covers, the teardrop-shaped indicators have just enough trim so as not to look totally stark.

simple ladder frame with near standard torsion-bar suspension and drum brakes, but as on Glöckler's cars (and on 356–1) the engine and transmission were turned round to give a mid-engined layout. Like Glöckler, Porsche went to coachbuilder Weidenhausen in Frankfurt for their lightweight, open two-seater body, and they added a coupé-type top for races such as Le Mans and the Carrera Panamericana.

The first 550 won first time out, at the Nürburgring in May 1953, and a couple of weeks later won the 1500 class at Le Mans. At the end of the year, two 550s ran in the Carrera, one leading its class until it dropped out, the other taking over to win.

‍ For 1954, it became even more specialised, with a stiffer chassis, redesigned rear suspension, a slightly cleaner shape – and the powerful new four-cylinder, four-cam, twin-plug 1500 engine, designed by Dr Ernst Fuhrmann.

With that combination, Hans Herrmann took a class win in the 1954 Carrera, and a remarkable third place overall – soon commemorated by the addition of the four-cam-engined 356 Carrera to the production model range. 550s had already won their classes in the 1954 Mille Miglia and at Le Mans, and late in the year they went on sale as Type 550S customer competition cars, many of them sold through the inevitable Hoffman for American sports car racing, where they soon became untouchable. It was apparently Hoffman, too, who dubbed the car Spyder; officially it was a 1500 RS, for *RennSport*, or racing sports car.

After another season and a half of success on both sides of the Atlantic, Porsche updated the car as the 550A, with more power (some 135bhp), a deeper, more complex spaceframe, revised rear suspension and a five-speed gearbox. To qualify

for homologation, more than 100 were built, which made it commercially important as well as being a racing test-bed; and, of course, it was even usable as a road car, albeit a rather raw one.

For 1958, the 550 Spyder gave way to a new derivative labelled the RSK, or 718 1500 Spyder. The K was a reference to the shape of a new front suspension unit, and the rear suspension had changed from torsion bars to coil springs, while power output had now gone beyond 140bhp. And by this point the sports cars were also forming the basis for a new Porsche line of single seaters, initially for the 1.5-litre F2 that was leading up to a 1.5-litre GP formula for 1961. In 1957 Porsche had entered a modified RS with full bodywork but only one seat (on the left) in the Nürburgring F2 race; Edgar Barth won with it. In 1968 Jean Behra used a version of the RSK, still with full bodywork but now with a single seat in the centre to win the Reims F2 race. And on that basis Porsche committed themselves to a pukka single-seater F2 car for 1959, though still based largely on RSK components.

The car was completed and tested just in time for its planned debut in the Monaco GP (as an F2 car running against mainly F1 opposition); and it was qualified quite respectably by Wolfgang von Trips who then unfortunately crashed on his second race lap. Porsche persevered, and by mid-1960 the F2 car was a winner, and with drivers like Stirling Moss, Graham Hill and Jo Bonnier the works team took the 1960 F2 constructors' championship.

That was their final step towards F1 in 1961, and they started the new formula with further uprated versions of the four-cylinder F2 cars while working on an eight-cylinder engine in anticipation of very strong opposition.

Even in the lightweight racing Spyders, Porsche managed to combine strict functionality in the cockpit (above) with a degree of comfort appropriate to long distance racing; the panel on the right gives easy access to the fuses.

Engine cooling was of paramount importance with the more highly stressed racing engines, and Porsche paid careful attention to getting as much air in, through the louvres in the car's flanks (left, centre), circulating, via the large horizontal engine fan (left, bottom), and out again, through the big open grilles in the tail (left).

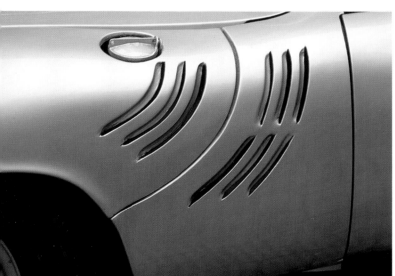

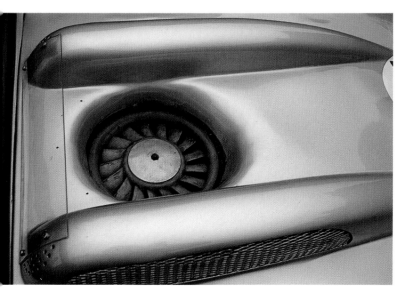

And in fact the opposition, for once, was too strong even for Porsche. Ferrari won the 1961 title largely by virtue of being far better prepared than anyone else, and by the time the eight-cylinder Porsche engine had appeared in 1962, the British BRM and Coventry-Climax-powered cars were getting into their stride and the Porsche was barely competitive. Dan Gurney drove a brilliant race to win the 1962 French GP at Rouen for Porsche, but at the end of the year they pulled out of GP racing for good.

But the lessons of F1 were by no means wasted, and the sports racing cars took another quantum leap. For 1960 and new rules which required cars virtually to road specification (including taller windscreens, a workable hood and notional luggage space), Porsche had turned the RSK into the RS60, and then the RS61. 'Grandmother' 718 047 was the classic continuation of the line. Built originally in 1961 with a four-cylinder four-cam engine, and driven to second place overall by Gurney and Bonnier on its debut in the Targa Florio, it was given a 1981cc, 210bhp version of the F1-type flat-eight during 1962 and started its remarkable run of success.

It took class wins in the Targa Florio and Nürburgring 1000km race and finished second overall in the endurance championship. And in between long and successful tours of duty in the USA it also began to dominate the European Hillclimb Championship, where four-cylinder models had already won in 1958, 1959, 1960 and 1961. Having done few rounds in 1962 because of other commitments, Porsche used the 718/8 regularly in 1963 and with up to 240bhp and a six-speed gearbox now available, Edgar Barth won the title very convincingly, and did the same again in 1964. By then though, Grandmother had a daughter, in the shape of the 904.

718/8 RS SPYDER SPECIFICATION

ENGINE
Flat-eight, air-cooled

CAPACITY
1981cc

BORE x STROKE
76.0 × 54.6mm

COMPRESSION RATIO
9.8:1

POWER
210bhp

VALVE GEAR
Two overhead camshafts per cylinder bank

FUEL SYSTEM
Four twin-choke downdraught Weber 38DCD carburettors

TRANSMISSION
Six-speed manual

FRONT SUSPENSION
Independent, by double wishbones, coil springs, telescopic dampers

REAR SUSPENSION
Independent, by double wishbones, coil springs, telescopic dampers

BRAKES
All discs

WHEELS
Bolt-on, steel/alloy disc

WEIGHT
1410lb (640kg)

MAXIMUM SPEED
162mph (260kph)

NUMBER MADE, DATES
Two eight-cylinder works cars, 1961–2

356C CARRERA 2000 COUPÉ

In 1950, to celebrate the opening of the Mexican section of the Pan American Highway, a spectacular motor race was conceived. It would follow the new road from one side of Mexico to the other, from Ciudad Juarez near El Paso in the north, to El Ocotal on the Guatemalan border, and it would be open to all-comers in any type of stock saloon car. The 2135-mile route would be split into five days racing and at the end of it there would be a massive prize fund, totalling over $38,000.

It was a great idea, enthusiastically backed by everyone from the car-mad Mexican president down; and against all the odds the great idea not only came to fruition in 1950, to open the 'super-highway', but it continued for each of the next five years, as one of the most punishing road races ever devised. It was known simply as the Carrera Panamericana: the Panamerican Road Race.

When it was opened up to sports cars, in 1951, what had started as an American-sedan dominated event soon attracted the attention of the classic European marques, who quickly

recognised it as a shop-window for US sales. So American manufacturers like Lincoln and Oldsmobile continued to dominate the stock classes, but the likes of Ferrari, Lancia and Mercedes now came to chase outright victory with full works teams. And, of course, they won.

The race grew bigger, more popular and faster every year, and in 1953 (when it counted towards the sports car championship) the winning Lancia *averaged* more than 138mph (222kph) for the long final leg, with speeds nudging 170mph (273kph) on closed public roads. In the early 1950s, Porsche couldn't compete for outright victory, but with their strong American market they couldn't ignore the Carrera for long either, and they had every chance of taking class wins in this race just as they were starting to do elsewhere.

In 1952, Prince Metternich won the 1500 class with a 356, and finished eighth overall in a race won by the mighty Mercedes 300SLs. In 1953, Porsche entered the first of the 550 Spyders, with 1500 pushrod engines, and took first and second places in the smaller sports car category, while a 356 won the

Although the overall shape of the 356C cars (right and overleaf) had barely changed at all from the high-bumper, high headlight 356B, there was a different wheel and hubcap design, prompted by the switch to disc brakes all round which the 356C had pioneered for production Porsches. Carrera wheels used a steel centre with an aluminium alloy rim.

Familiar shapes continued in the nose of the 356C Carrera (left), with the slightly raked-back headlamps, and in particular the smooth curve of the bonnet line, showing increasingly distant, but still clearly recognisable, V W Beetle genealogy.

production class again. Then in 1954, Porsche entered 550s with a new four-cam, four-cylinder race engine, which took Hans Herrmann to a dominant class win and a quite outstanding third place overall, beaten only by the Ferraris of Umberto Maglioli and Phil Hill.

Sadly, that was the end of the Panamerican Road Race; after a string of fatalities involving both drivers and spectators, it was finally abandoned. But as one legend came to an end, another was about to be born, in the Porsches named for the great race.

The first of the line appeared at the Frankfurt Show in September 1955, as the 356A 1500GS Carrera. The thinking behind it was brilliantly simple; take the latest 356 and blend it with an only mildly detuned version of the four-cam engine from the 550 Spyder, to produce the fastest Porsche road car thus far – and name it to celebrate the Mexican race. Porsche thought they could sell it in a limited series, possibly fifty or at most 100 cars, but once again they were in for a big surprise.

Maybe there was no real surprise, though, in the fact that the Carrera was created; the four-cam flat-four was a very simple transplant into the 356 shell, so it was too good a chance to miss.

The engine was the key. It had been mooted as early as 1952, when Ferry Porsche had pondered just how much power could be coaxed from the air-cooled four. The task of finding out was given to Dr Ernst Fuhrmann, who redesigned the engine virtually from scratch, keeping only the air-cooled, horizontally-opposed layout and the latest 1498cc capacity. His type 547 engine used a Hirth crankshaft with roller main and big-end bearings, and it had dry sump lubrication, but its biggest advance was in the cylinder heads and valve operation.

Gone were the single central camshaft and pushrods, and in their place was an elegant layout with two widely-spaced overhead camshafts per cylinder bank. A gear-drive at the clutch end of the crankshaft drove a short shaft below the crank, from which the drive was taken by a train of bevel gears and short shafts between each pair of cylinders to drive the lower (exhaust) cams on each cylinder bank. Another pair of short shafts with bevel gears then transferred drive vertically to the inlet cams, and finally by rockers to the inclined valves; by mounting finger-type rockers on threaded pillars, Fuhrmann solved the problem of valve adjustability; the wide valve angle allowed an almost perfect hemispherical combustion chamber shape above high-domed pistons, and room for two spark plugs per cylinder – fed by two distributors on the ends of the inlet cams. A pair of twin choke downdraught carburettors gave each cylinder its own choke, feeding almost vertically down through very short inlet ports, through the cylinders in classic cross-flow mode, and out through equally short, straight exhaust parts below the heads.

It was a superb design and even as first tested, over Easter 1953 (three years to the day after the first Stuttgart-built 356 was completed), it slightly improved on Fuhrmann's notional target – giving 112bhp on the test bed.

While it was starting its racing career, Porsche put one in Ferry Porsche's own 356 during 1954, and later in a 356 Cabrio. When the 356A range was launched, with uprated suspension with anti-roll bars, and wider wheels and tyres, it was an ideal basis for a production version of the car, and so the Carrera was born.

Porsche offered two versions, first the fully-trimmed 356A Carrera 1500GS and then (from early 1957) the lighter, less elaborate 1500GT. Both were detuned from the race engines, but not by much, and they were still individually hand-built. The GS gave 110bhp and the GT 115, while the GT had plastic windows, alloy bonnet, doors and engine cover, plus Spyder front brakes. They were extremely expensive, but they were capable of almost 125mph (200kph), and by far the fastest

The twin engine cooling grilles (above left) and the squared-off engine cover shape above the higher bumpers (above) had continued from the 356B, and even if you couldn't read the script, the Carrera was distinguished by its twin tailpipes emerging near the centre rather than below the bumper overriders.

The stylised script (above) reveals a Carrera 2, fastest and best developed of all the 356 family. By the 356C, dash-mounted heater controls (left) had changed V W-style knobs for sliding levers. Quarter lights (left, below) had reappeared on the 356B, and continued on the 356Cs.

thing in their class. They didn't shout about it though – they never did – and almost the only external recognition points were gold 'Carrera' scripts on the engine covers and front wings, plus twin exhausts.

For 1958, capacity started at 1498cc but was soon increased in line with the top of the comparable pushrod range, to 1588cc – although the four-cam engines then reverted to plain bearings rather than the expensive and fussy roller-crank type and maximum power was almost unchanged. The latest body modifications also found their way onto the Carrera, and another variant was offered – a 'hardtop coupé' by Karmann, with a short roofline not unlike that of the cabriolet's soft-top, sold in very limited numbers.

By the time the Carrera progressed into 356B guise at the Frankfurt Show late in 1959, sales were already approaching 700 units, startling when compared to Porsche's original thoughts of fifty to 100!

The 1600 engines were steadily uprated, mainly for reliability, through 1960 and 1961, with changes to carburation, lubrication, bearings and ignition, and the Carrera introduced 12-volt electrics, but the biggest and last change was to come at the Frankfurt Show in September 1961. It was the 356B-bodied Carrera 2000GS, with capacity increased to 1966cc, and power to 130bhp. In April 1962 it went on sale as the Carrera 2, the fastest of all the 356 Carrera family. It had Porsche's first production disc brakes, and a reputation for needing a skilled and brave driver to get the most from it now it had this much power.

It survived to the end of the 356 line, but good as it was it was obviously running out of its time. Racing was growing too specialised for even a wild production model like this, and the 911 was about to offer a new start. Briefly, the Carrera was an anachronism, but it had also become an important part of Porsche legend.

356C CARRERA 2000 COUPÉ SPECIFICATION

ENGINE
Flat-four, air-cooled

CAPACITY
1966cc

BORE x STROKE
92.0 x 74.0mm

COMPRESSION RATIO
9.8:1

POWER
130bhp

VALVE GEAR
Two overhead camshafts per cylinder bank

FUEL SYSTEM
Two twin-choke downdraught Weber 46IDM2 carburettors

TRANSMISSION
Four-speed manual

FRONT SUSPENSION
Independent, by trailing arms, transverse torsion bars, telescopic dampers, anti-roll bar

REAR SUSPENSION
Independent, by swing axles, transverse torsion bars, telescopic dampers

BRAKES
All discs

WHEELS
Bolt-on, steel disc

WEIGHT
c.2060lb (935kg)

MAXIMUM SPEED
125mph (200kph)

NUMBER MADE, DATES
126, 1963–4

904 CARRERA
GTS COUPÉ

How many series-built cars have scored back-to-back wins in the 2-litre GT class of the world sports car championship, won the Targa Florio outright, and won on handicap in the punishing Tour de France, taken class wins in the Nürburgring 1000km and Reims 24-hour, *and* finished second on a snowbound Monte Carlo Rally – yet also, at a pinch, been usable as a road car?

The answer, of course, is just one: the start of a new line of Porsche sports racers. Nominally it was the Carrera GTS, but to the factory it was the 904, and that's how everyone remembers it.

Porsche announced it in December 1963, for homologation as a 2-litre GT for 1964 – which would require a minimum of 100 cars to be built. Porsche kept the first batch of six for works use, delivered customer cars to the USA in January 1964 and duly built the requisite 100 for homologation by April – plus an extra twenty, of which four were left in component form, as a spares pool.

They intended the 904, above all, to be a reliable and durable car; it was built, they said, 'for real long distance races, not artificial sprints'. So they built it strong, and with hindsight you could say that they built it rather heavy.

It followed the now familiar mid-engined two-seater pattern set for Porsche competition cars by the 550s and the 718s; but in terms of construction it was a complete departure from anything they had done before, using a glassfibre body-shell bonded onto a relatively simple, fabricated chassis.

The main strength came from two deep but quite slim box-section side members, set apart at almost the full width of the car through the length of the cockpit, but angled inwards at front and rear, stopping virtually in line with the wheelbase. The side members were linked by hoop-like cross members at the extreme front and rear of the chassis, which provided the suspension pick-ups; at the rear, the gearbox projected through the middle of the hoop. There were further box-section cross members under the front edges of the seats, in line with the gearlever, and across the back of the cockpit under the seat backs; and there was a simple platform floor, with no particular centre rib.

The suspension owed its layout to the not very successful F1 cars of 1962, modified for the needs of a heavier car, and also to suit production in much larger numbers than the single-seaters. It used upper and lower wishbones at the front, with concentric coil-spring/damper units and an anti-roll bar; and a

Butzi Porsche styled the mid-engined 904 (left) in double quick time and without compromises, and he reckoned it to be his most successful exercise ever; although it was designed primarily as a racing car, it was genuinely roadworthy too – if not very refined.

The 904 brought plastic body panels to Porsche for the first time, and handsome though the 904 coupé was, you don't need to look too closely at the very variable panel fits (left and overleaf) to see that the body builders still had a bit to learn; inconsistent thickness meant the shell was overweight too.

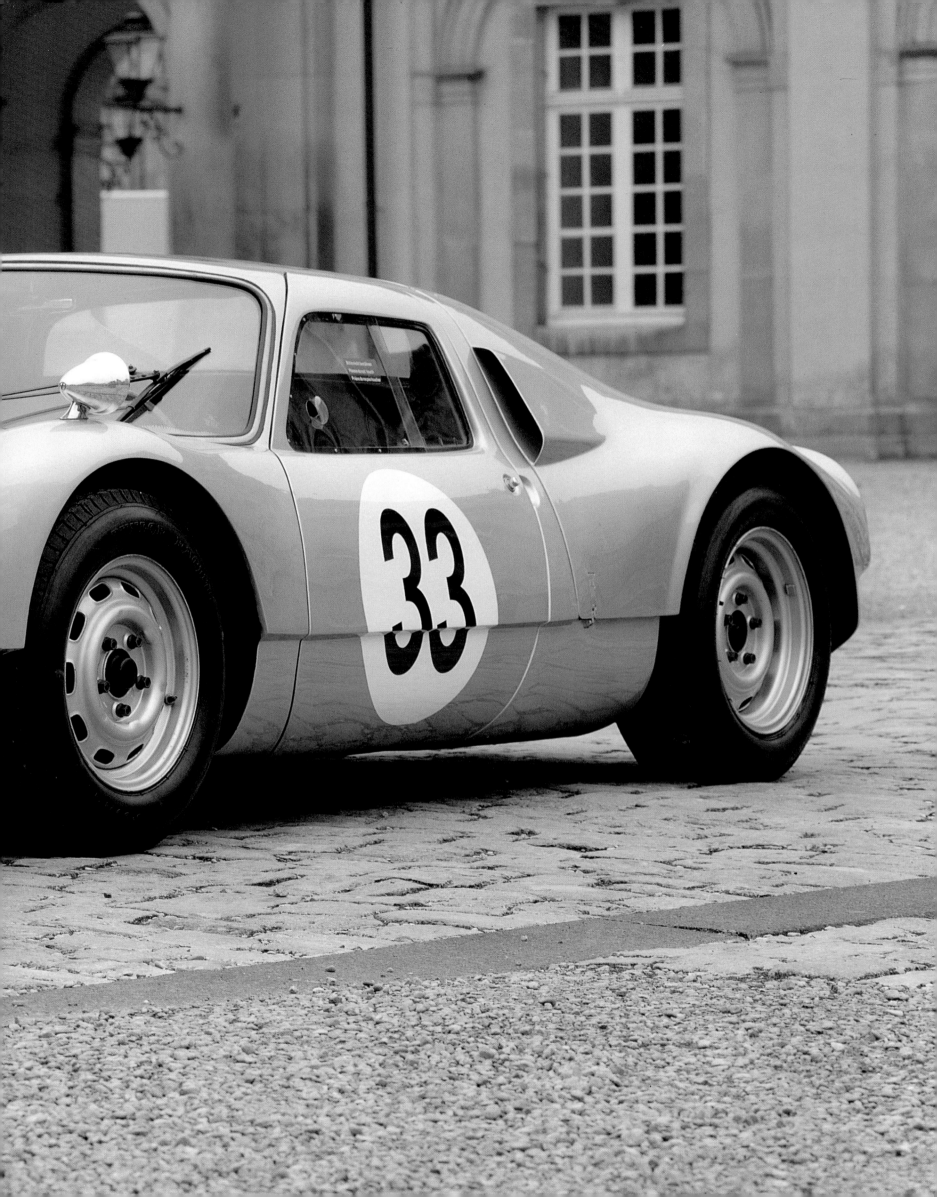

four-link layout at the rear, with upper and lower radius arms, a reversed upper wishbone, and a lower link, again with coil-spring/dampers and an anti-roll bar.

The brakes were discs all round and the steering used a new ZF rack and pinion. With just two turns lock-to-lock it was very quick, but not always quick enough to catch the notoriously easy-to-spin car should the driver overstep (as was always tempting) its very fine limits.

The shell was in 'Pantal', a BASF glassfibre clone, and was moulded for Porsche by the Heinkel works. It was bonded directly onto the steel chassis, and contributed to the overall stiffness of the structure; but it had its problems. Porsche had never used the material before, and nor had many other manufacturers, so the 904 appeared with quite a good finish but very variable panel fits. A major problem was that the panels were of inconsistent thickness, and tended to err on the heavy side. Some early works cars were 350lb and more over the homologated minimum, and although Porsche promised that customer cars would weigh no more than 1540lb (about half way between Porsche's heaviest and the homologated minimum) the 904 always had a weight problem.

Butzi Porsche styled the 904, and he always loved the 904; in 1966 he told *Road & Track*, 'It was my favourite because I did it alone and there wasn't this fight to change it or make it newer. It was designed and finished. Time was very short. I didn't have a *free* hand but it had to appear so soon after the clay model there was really no time for interference . . .'

The body mouldings also comprised most of the interior of the 904, and the seat upholstery simply slotted into the moulded recesses of the back wall of the cockpit. Customers were offered a choice of seat sizes and shapes, but the seats themselves were fixed and the pedals and steering column were adjustable. For the driver it was a comfortable car, even over long distances. It had a full complement of instruments – plus things like road-legal lights, indicators, and washers/wipers – and it had acceptable visibility, even to the rear; but passenger accommodation was a 'notional' requirement, demanded for homologation, so the right-side footwell was largely filled with battery box, and upholstery was minimal. Nor was a 904 trimmed as a roadgoing car, and it certainly wasn't soundproofed as one; it was *very* noisy inside.

That was part and parcel of the character of the four-cylinder, four-cam Spyder-type engine, which was specified as standard once it was accepted that the 911-type six wouldn't be available in time. It was the final, 1966cc version, with big bores and short stroke, and in standard customer specification it typically used two twin-choke downdraught Weber carburettors and a compression ratio of 9.8:1. It would rev willingly but incredibly noisily to a 7200rpm red-line and Porsche quoted peaks of 180bhp and 145lb ft of torque, with the very latest engines claiming as much as 195bhp. There *was* such a thing as a roadgoing option, with less extreme cams, air cleaners and a degree of silencing, and that offered 155bhp and 124lb ft of torque. Porsche themselves also tried the eight-cylinder F1-type engine in the 904, although it was never a serious possibility for series production, and although the option of using a 911-based six-cylinder engine was more realistic it was largely left to the after-market.

The single, pantograph-type windscreen wiper (above) was a typical bit of minimalist racing design, and the style of the numerous air intakes which were dotted around the 904 shell (left) varied from car to car, largely dictated by the individual car's main racing requirements.

Prominent air scoops just aft of the doors (left) fed cool air into the engine compartment, and in this case the filler cap is for the dry sump's oil tank. The door catches were simple push-buttons, with space for the pulls neatly recessed into the rear bodywork.

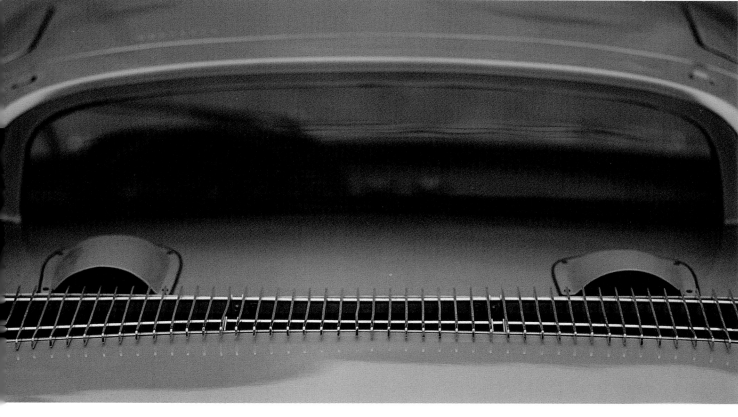

The deeply recessed rear
window (left) made room for
a large, flat rear deck and
some more engine
compartment air intake area.
The 904 was properly mid-
engined (left, below) with the
flat-four ahead of the gearbox
and the line of the rear axle.

Its racing career was short but sweet. It lasted just two seasons, but the 904 dominated its class in both of them. On its debut at Sebring in 1964 the front running car retired but another survived to win the prototype class, because the 904 wasn't yet homologated as a GT. In April, it scored that famous Targa Florio win. At Le Mans, both eight-cylinder works cars retired, having run as high as second, but all five four-cylinder entries survived, to finish 7–8–10–11–12 overall. A third place overall in the Nürburgring 1000km and third to sixth places overall in the Tour de France (including first and second on handicap) helped Porsche clinch the 2-litre GT championship.

The 904 repeated that in 1965, but its most astonishing result was in the snowbound Monte Carlo Rally, where Eugen Böhringer tigered his way to second place in what must have seemed the unlikeliest of cars to survive the conditions when only twenty-two of the 237 starters did so.

In the end, the 904 was overtaken by new rules, and because Porsche had learned how to do the same thing even better. With its box-section chassis and glassfibre body, the 904 was strong but it was heavy, and difficult to work on when damaged. And the four-cam flat-four was at the end of its development, while the flat-six which had become available with the birth of the 911 was only at the beginning – and already capable of producing more power than the faithful old four-cam ever could.

So the 904 was superseded by the 906 Carrera 6, with spaceframe chassis, lighter and more aerodynamic bodywork, and a 210bhp derivative of the 911 engine. It was ultra-successful in its own right, of course, and sixty-seven were built. It won the Targa Florio in 1966, and much else, but it would be hard to argue that it had the versatility of the 904, and it certainly didn't qualify as a road car. In that respect, the 904 perhaps remains unique.

**904 CARRERA GTS COUPÉ
SPECIFICATION**

ENGINE
Flat-four, air-cooled

CAPACITY
1966cc

BORE x STROKE
92.0 x 74.0mm

COMPRESSION RATIO
9.8:1

POWER
195bhp

VALVE GEAR
Two overhead camshafts per cylinder bank

FUEL SYSTEM
Two twin-choke downdraught Weber 46IDM carburettors

TRANSMISSION
Five-speed manual

FRONT SUSPENSION
Independent, by double wishbones, coil springs, telescopic dampers, anti-roll bar

REAR SUSPENSION
Independent, by upper and lower radius arms, reversed upper wishbone, lower link, coil springs, telescopic dampers, anti-roll bar

BRAKES
All discs

WHEELS
Bolt-on, light-alloy discs

WEIGHT
1540lb (699kg)

MAXIMUM SPEED
c.160mph (257kph)

NUMBER MADE, DATES
120, 1963–4

911 COUPÉ

On September 1963, at the Frankfurt Motor Show, one of the great cars of all time was introduced to the public. It was the model with which Porsche intended shortly to replace the astonishingly successful and still highly regarded 356, and it was new and improved in virtually every respect. It appeared at Frankfurt as the Porsche 901, but before it went into production the following year it had been re-designated, after Peugeot had claimed sovereignty over the three-digit number with a central zero; so the 901 became the 911 and a legend was born.

Ferry Porsche once described it as 'a second beginning for Porsche', but if the 911's design was all-new, the philosophy was entirely familiar. As ever, Porsche had thought in terms of power to weight ratio, not just power alone, and the simple tenets that had saved weight and complexity for the Beetle and the 356 held just as firmly for the 911.

Or at least they did once Ferry Porsche had stamped his authority on the design and reaffirmed what, in his tutored opinion, Porsches were all about.

In 1960, Porsche turnover had passed the DM100 million level for the first time ever, the company had just expanded into its No. 3 works in Stuttgart, a massive new development centre was under construction at Weissach, and the 356 was near the peak of its sales success; but Porsche knew that the model couldn't go on for ever. For a while they looked at 356-based options, and especially at four-seaters, and they built prototypes of everything from four-cylinder, four-seater saloon to coupé to cabrio – proving along the way that they could build a bigger car with very little weight penalty; but there was something about a four-seater that just wasn't Porsche, and eventually Ferry Porsche ruled that the new car had to be *really* new, with better accommodation than the 356 but without getting into saloon car territory, with as much or more power and performance than the quickest of the 356s but with more refinement and, especially, less noise.

Fundamentally, he wanted a compact, lightweight, 2 + 2 sports car, with a six-cylinder engine. True, the pushrod four-cylinder engines, having grown from 1100 to 1600cc, and

A new look for Porsche, after fourteen years of the 356. While still having some of the styling cues of the 356, the new 911 (right and overleaf) had a more modern, sharper edged look; drawn originally by Butzi Porsche and productionised by Komenda, it looks as fresh today as it did in 1963.

Practicality was one of the main themes of the 911's design parameters, and as well as the space to carry a full set of golf clubs, that meant a bit more room inside (left) and with better trim and equipment levels – but it was still a sports car.

from 40bhp to 115, had reached the end of their development anyway; and the 130bhp four-cam four-cylinder Carrera unit was something of an anachronism – a racing design that was too expensive and too noisy to have any place in the next generation road car. But perhaps more than anything, six cylinders would finally lay to rest the notion of a Porsche being little more than a pumped-up VW, and open the door for Porsche to grow as a marque in its own right. So development started on engine type 745.

It was the first six-cylinder engine Porsche had built, and the first wholly Porsche production engine. Initially, they schemed a 2-litre pushrod six, closely related to the old four, intending to tackle the noise problem by using oil-cooled cylinder barrels while retaining the familiar air-cooled heads. Adding weight, however, was anathema to Porsche, so the design was scrapped.

Next, the engineers juggled with camshaft position and valve layout, to balance performance with compactness and the obsession with low noise. There was another pushrod engine, but with two cams in the bottom of the crankcase; then one with one cam above and one cam below, with both inlet and exhaust valves inclined. Intending originally to shoehorn some luggage space into the tail of the car above the engine (space was another obsession), they tried sidedraught carbs outboard of the rocker covers, but that made the engine too wide, and it was still considered too noisy anyway, so that was another reject.

One thing did survive from that stage: bore and stroke were fixed at 80 × 66mm for a capacity of 1991cc, with the scope to grow through 2.2 and possibly as far as 2.5 litres in time. The pushrod layout was scrapped, though, and work started on adding single overhead cams, driven by chains – which were cheaper and quieter than the gears of the Carrera-type engine and better proven than the new belt-drives which were just appearing.

Naturally, construction was mainly in light alloys, with a forged, seven-bearing crankshaft (plus an extra bearing at the timing-gear end) and steel rods. The crankcase was split vertically along the crank line, the individual barrels had square fins and cast-iron liners, and the individual heads had inclined valves with sodium-filled exhausts. The cams ran in one-piece alloy cam boxes which tied the top end of the engine together, and carburation was originally by two down-draught, triple-choke carburettors. It was cooled by a single large fan, belt-driven at a little over engine speed, and while satisfying the quest for refinement and low noise it equalled the power output of the race-bred four-cylinder Carrera engine, with 130bhp at 6100rpm and 129lb ft of torque at 4200rpm.

As engine type 901/01 it would be the heart of a completely new car that was taking shape simultaneously – and once

A full-length front lid (top, left) offered usefully more luggage space and a worthwhile reduction in drag. The first six-cylinder production engine (top, right) was as difficult to see as any of the fours had been. Steel wheels (above) were original staple option.

The opening front quarter-windows carried over from the late 356s to the early 911s (far left) but as part of a significantly bigger overall glass area. The flap by the door mirror and radio aerial (left) covers the fuel filler cap and is released from the dashboard.

again subject to some very firm dictates from Ferry Porsche.

He wanted the car to be roomier and more civilised than the 356, but he didn't want it to be significantly bigger or heavier. He rejected the idea of the full four-seater early on, but did agree that a 2 + 2 would be correct. And he had a fine starting point for a modern but characteristically Porsche look in a styling exercise drawn up by his eldest son, Ferdinand Alexander, who had worked with Komenda in the design department since 1957.

'Butzi', as Ferdinand was known, had already drawn more or less what the 911 turned out to be, but there was to be a bout of political in-fighting around the design studio before it made it into production. The style was Butzi's, but it was Komenda who would have to turn it into an engineering design for production, and in three successive prototype variants working towards that end, Komenda showed his

personal prejudice towards a true four-seater, and the elegant shell grew progressively larger.

Now Ferry Porsche intervened, with the pivotal decisions that made the 911 what it is. He decreed that it would *not* be a four-seater, that its wheelbase would be no more than 2.2 m, that it would have the all-round torsion bar suspension with struts at the front and semi-trailing arms at the rear, all disc brakes, the overhead-cam flat-six engine, and a five-speed gearbox. The legend goes that he also insisted that, for all its compactness, the 911 coupé should be roomy enough to carry a full set of golf clubs.

And when Komenda continued to cite practical difficulties in engineering the style down to size in a unitary shell, Ferry Porsche took Butzi's original drawing to Reutter (which Porsche would own from early 1964) and had *them* prepare the engineering plans, with the style virtually unchanged. The wheelbase was only around five inches longer than on the 356, the car itself was only some six inches longer overall, and actually narrower, but much more roomy and with usefully bigger doors and windows.

The yellow show car was well received in Frankfurt and later by testers, who loved the additional performance even if they still quaked slightly at the familiar rear-engined handling traits. There was also the normal proviso that some Porsche aficionados couldn't see the point in replacing the 356, but it was almost a year anyway before the new car went into production, in August 1964. The type number had changed to 911, the two carburettors had changed to six single-choke units, and the 356-type dashboard had been replaced by a five-dial one whose layout is familiar even today. A good deal else is still familiar too, but through some twenty-eight years and well over a quarter of a million cars the 911 has simply grown better and better. Even Porsche, though, could hardly have imagined in 1963 that the car would make it into the mid-1990s, and still be going strong.

911 COUPÉ SPECIFICATION

ENGINE
Flat-six, air-cooled

CAPACITY
1991cc

BORE x STROKE
80.0 x 66.0mm

COMPRESSION RATIO
9.0:1

POWER
130bhp

VALVE GEAR
Single overhead camshaft per cylinder bank

FUEL SYSTEM
Six single-choke downdraught Solex 40PI carburettors

TRANSMISSION
Five-speed manual

FRONT SUSPENSION
Independent, by MacPherson struts, lower wishbones, longitudinal torsion bars, telescopic dampers, anti-roll bar

REAR SUSPENSION
Independent, by semi-trailing arms, transverse torsion bars, telescopic dampers

BRAKES
All discs

WHEELS
Bolt-on, steel discs

WEIGHT
2380lb (1080kg)

MAXIMUM SPEED
130mph (210kph)

NUMBER MADE, DATES
10,723 (including Targas), 1964-7

912 COUPÉ

When Porsche began to replace the 356 with the 911, in 1964, they improved on the old car in every respect bar one; as promised, the 911 would be quicker yet easier to drive, it was more comfortable and more refined, and especially it was more roomy, both for passengers and their luggage. The one catch was that in making this substantial leap in sophistication, the new model had also taken a major jump in price. As launched, the 911 was around 30 per cent more expensive than any late model 356 except the very specialised, 2-litre, 130bhp, four-cam-engined Carrera, and that wasn't easy to ignore.

The American *Car & Driver* magazine, for instance, commented in 1966 that 'At almost $6500, the 911 is more than a Corvette, less than a Ferrari, and within not too many dollars of being a mighty expensive car.' They hadn't been the first to notice, and Porsche were well aware that there was a danger of pricing the faithful customers who had got the marque off the ground off even the bottom rung of the Porsche ladder. They couldn't afford to do that, and although they intended to run on with the 356 for a while, to use up stocks and satisfy orders,

nor could they reasonably keep selling the older car alongside the 911. So they needed a compromise; and the compromise was the 912.

It *looked* like a 911, which helped buyers-on-a-budget to choose it without feeling too second-class; it had all the benefits of space and drivability; and it was mechanically similar enough to the 911 for Porsche to enjoy all the benefits of cost saving through improved volume, but with only minimal investment – on all of which bases it seemed to be a very elegant solution. And, for a while at least, it really was.

Like all the best Porsche ideas, it was very simple: take the basic 911, replace the most expensive bits with something more modest, preferably off-the-shelf, and sell on the strength of shared reputation. So the 912 evolved as a 911 with a bit less trim, a four-speed gearbox as standard, and – the masterstroke – the 1.6-litre, four-cylinder, pushrod engine carried over from the last of the 356 line, the 1600SC.

It wasn't in the same league as the new and instantly acclaimed flat-six, of course, but there was life in the old four yet. For the 912 it was virtually identical to the way it had last

There was very little externally to distinguish the 912 (left) from the higher-priced 911, which was exactly as Porsche intended. Steel wheels were standard on the 912, for reasons of cost (overleaf), but the optional five-spoke alloys offered later gave the 912 even more of a 911 look.

With shared bodyshells, the 912 naturally retained neat 911 features like the flip-up filler flap in the front wing (below), released from inside the car by a simple knob on the dash, and with an 'apron' to stop splashes staining the bodywork.

appeared in the 356SC, with a capacity of 1582cc and a pair of twin-choke downdraught Solex carburettors. It was slightly detuned from the 1600SC's 95bhp, to give the same 90bhp as the earlier Super 90 model, but the torque spread was improved, to give a 90lb ft peak at 3600rpm, and with at least 87lb ft available all the way from 2800 to 5000rpm.

That apart, there was little mechanical difference between 911 and 912, with both cars sharing the new strut-front, semi-trailing-arm-rear, all-independent torsion-bar suspension, the new disc brakes all round, rack and pinion steering, and 12-volt electrics. The 912 had a four-speed manual gearbox as standard, but a closer ratio five-speed was offered as a reasonably priced option, and every tester recommended it as giving the entry-level car perfectly acceptable performance even with limited power.

It was helped a little bit in that respect by being lighter than the 911, because the delete options which had pared cost had also mostly pared weight. The engine, of course, was lighter, and there was less trim – though certainly not so little as to make the 912 feel cheap or spartan. It had similar reclining seats to those in the 911, for instance (and a choice of materials, in cloth, vinyl or leather), it had three-speed wipers, a heated rear 'screen, and reversing lights, but – initially at least – it only had the three-dial dash of the 356 rather than the five-dial one of the 911, and it had lost the 911's wood trim. So although it was a couple of hundred pounds heavier than the 356, it was about 130lb lighter than the 911, and acceptably nimble. Most testers reckoned on about 115mph (185kph) and 0–60mph (0–96kph) in say 11½ seconds – respectively about 10mph and three seconds adrift of a 911 and a bit quicker than a 356 on top speed thanks to the better shape.

The bonus was that it could sell for some 25 per cent less than a 911, and very little more than the 356SC which if finally replaced completely during 1965.

It looked just about identical to the 911, it was economical to run (with around 25mpg fairly easily attainable), and (outright performance apart) it was just as much improved over the 356 in its road manners as was the 911 – the lighter engine, if anything, giving the 912 even better handling balance than the first six-cylinder cars. When the Targa option was offered for the 911, it was offered for the 912, too, and the badging was always subtle enough to play down the differences, while the build quality was everything Porsche buyers had come to expect.

The formula worked, and in 1966 two thirds of Porsche's total 911/912 output was of the four-cylinder model.

Little or nothing about the 912 would distinguish it from a contemporaneous 911. The nose of the 912 (above left) was identical even down to retaining the bumper overriders which some manufacturers might have dropped to save pfennigs. The slant of the headlamps, the neat air intake grilles and the combined turn indicator and parking light units (above) were all pure 911.

The real difference between 912 and 911 was below the familiar tail (left), where lurked the 1.6-litre flat-four engine from the last of the 356s, rather than the 2-litre flat-six from the first of the 911s. A four-speed gearbox was standard, but five speeds were a popular option. The elegant lines of the 911 (below left) came as standard even in this cut-price sibling.

which said what a lot of other people were obviously starting to think; they acknowledged that the general concept of the cut-price model was still fine, but they had to observe that, 'The Porsche 911/912 was designed around the 911's six-cylinder engine, and the 912's little Four doesn't seem up the job. What the 911 does easily, the 912 can only strain for, and although its 102hp, 1.6-liter engine is willing, it can't hold a candle to the 148hp 2.0-liter Six. The basic car is an elegant concept, and squeaking by with the old VW-related engine seems too much of an economy move – like a Rolls-Royce with an Austin engine.'

The problem was that as the 911 had grown steadily more powerful, the 912's output had stood still, and the gap had widened. The 911 was given fuel injection from 1968, but the 912 stayed on carburettors and 90bhp (the 102bhp quoted by *Car & Driver* was the usual American SAE figure); and when the size of the six-cylinder engine was increased for the first time, to 2.2 litres for 1970, the disparity between 911 and 912 was finally too big for all but the most sanguine or the least sensitive to gloss over; the days of the 912 were numbered.

By then, in any case, Porsche (in partnership with VW) had conceived what initially seemed a better way of filling the awkward gap below the 911, in the guise of the joint-venture 914 family, and the 912 was dropped in 1970, without too much dissent by this stage, except for owners and aficionados of this elegant little car.

In one final twist, though, the 912 made a brief and decidedly low-key reappearance in 1976, in the guise of the 912E – which was a simply-trimmed 911 with the VW-based, 2-litre, fuel-injected flat-four from the 914 – the car which had replaced the original 912 six years earlier! The 912E lasted just one season, until both it and the mid-engined 914s were replaced by Porsche's next attempt at creating an entry-level range – the 924.

To an extent, the 912 also kept pace with running changes. In 1967 it was given the 911's five-dial dash; in 1968 it gained the same longer wheelbase, longer semi-trailing arms, and wider track, for improved weight distribution and less tail-happiness. It didn't get the 911's revised front struts, but the new five-spoke alloy wheels were offered as an option, so it could still look just like a well-specified 911 – and other options included air conditioning, an electric sunroof and tinted glass.

Unfortunately, the one area where it didn't even keep up was in performance, and that began to hurt. In a summary of the 912 in January 1968, it was *Car & Driver* magazine again

912 COUPÉ SPECIFICATION

ENGINE
Flat-four, air-cooled

CAPACITY
1582cc

BORE x STROKE
82.5 × 74.0mm

COMPRESSION RATIO
9.3:1

POWER
90bhp

VALVE GEAR
Single central camshafts, pushrods

FUEL SYSTEM
Two twin-choke downdraught Solex 40PJJ4 carburettors

TRANSMISSION
Four-speed manual (five-speed optional)

FRONT SUSPENSION
Independent, by MacPherson struts, lower wishbones, longitudinal torsion bars, telescopic dampers, anti-roll bar

REAR SUSPENSION
Independent, by semi-trailing arms, transverse torsion bars, telescopic dampers

BRAKES
All discs

WHEELS
Bolt-on, steel discs

WEIGHT
2130lb (966kg)

MAXIMUM SPEED
115mph (185kph)

NUMBER MADE, DATES
30,300 (incl. Targas), 1965–8

914, 914/6

The late 1960s were mostly good times for Porsche. The 911 was handsomely justifying Porsche's huge investment in it; works and customer competition cars were dominating top class sports car racing; and among the many projects in hand on the design side was the potentially lucrative task of creating a Beetle successor for VW. A nagging problem kept recurring, though: there was still an awkward gap below the 911 for a true entry-level Porsche, well below the 911's far from entry-level price.

For a while, the four-cylinder 912 had filled the role quite well; but as 911 and 912 performance drifted further apart, no one was fooled any more, and the 912 was increasingly seen as a poor relation. What Porsche needed wasn't something pretending to be a 911 and no longer doing it very well, they needed a second, lower-priced, high-volume line, with a

strong enough personality to stand on its own; and they needed it soon.

Knowing *what* they needed, however, was only a small part of Porsche's problem; so soon after bank-rolling the 911, funding another new car (and finding the space to build it in the sort of numbers that would make it work) was a much bigger one. But there was a familiar light at the end of the tunnel.

While Porsche were trying to keep the faith with their less wealthy stalwarts, VW had their own dilemma; the nearest thing they had to a sports car was the pretty but hardly rapid Beetle-based Karmann Ghia coupé; and pending the arrival of their next generation they were paying the penalty of becoming synonymous only with the Beetle itself, and utility motoring for the masses. Given the close relationship between

The 914's styling (overleaf) started life on a front-engined BMW project, but was heavily revised by Butzi Porsche. The car's Targa-type roll-over hoop (right) created a new and admirably versatile roof style, which soon found its way onto other Porsche models.

Even when the 914 was the six-cylinder version and powered by Porsche, the badging (below) still acknowledged Porsche's role in the project.

Porsche and V W, the solution wasn't too difficult to see – in a family of joint venture sports cars which could bear either V W or Porsche badges, depending on specification, price and market.

So V W commissioned Porsche to design a sports car, based for V W purposes around the 1.7-litre fuel-injected flat-four engine from the 411 saloon, and which at the same time would offer Porsche a platform on which to build a six-cylinder variant for their own purposes – to a fairly flexible, 'gentleman's agreement' between Ferry Porsche and V W boss Heinrich Nordhoff.

With generous access to the V W parts bins, and a decent budget, Porsche went for a mid-engined layout, thus demonstrating that they were less dogmatic than some of their staunchest fans chose to believe. Those who protested that 'real' Porsches should be rear-engined, in the image of the 356 and the 911, had presumably overlooked mid-engined competition cars from the 550 Spyder onwards, through the 904, 906, 908 and most recently the awesome 917 – all of them predating the new joint venture. Maybe they'd even forgotten that the first Porsche of all had a V W engine ahead of its rear axle.

And if the mid-engined layout raised a few eyebrows, the styling raised many more. It was based on work started by an industrial design company, Gugelot, for a putative *front-engined* BMW sports car, but taken over and revised by Butzi Porsche – he who had styled the 911. More people called it ugly than called it pretty, but it was undeniably functional. It was low and wide, with the versatility of a fixed Targa-type hoop around the rear window, and a removable roof panel. It had the first pop-up headlamps to be seen on a Porsche, limited service access to the mid-mounted engine via the rear deck, and a generous amount of luggage space both fore and aft. It was seven inches (177mm) shorter than a 911, but seven

The big bumpers (above left) were dictated by the need to be saleable in the USA with minimal changes, and pop-up headlights were used for the first time on a Porsche. The interior (above) was fine for two but no more. Five-spoked alloy wheels on the 914/6 (left) were one of the stronger Porsche hallmarks.

inches longer in the wheelbase, which suggests how short the overhangs were – and such overhangs as there were were largely the big, clumsy bumpers demanded by US legislation.

It was strictly a two-seater, and the four- and six-cylinder models would be distinguishable principally by different wheels, a vinyl covering for the 914/6's roof and Targa bar, and minor bits of chrome strip and badging. Engines aside, the two versions would be very similar and borrow heavily from the 911. Front suspension was pure 911, with lower

Without the Targa bar, the
914 (left), in spite of its mid-
engined layout, would have
looked almost ordinary, but
Porsche didn't get to be
Porsche by following the herd.
If nothing else, the 914 was
both versatile and
impressively practical.

wishbones and struts, plus torsion bars; rear suspension was simplified semi-trailing-link, but with coil springs rather than torsion bars, and there were no anti-roll bars on these lower, lighter cars. Steering was by rack and pinion, à la 911, and there were disc brakes all round – solid 411-derived ones for the 914, ventilated 911 fronts and solid 912 rears for the 914/6, which also offered detail niceties like a full complement of 911 instruments, three-speed wipers and minor refinements that the cheaper car lacked. Both variants offered a choice of five-speed, all-syncro manual gearbox (with ratios to suit the appropriate engine), or Porsche's four-speed Sportmatic semi-automatic.

As for engines, the Bosch-injected four-cylinder had iron barrels but aluminium heads and crankcase, and a capacity of 1679cc. It had a very short stroke but also had a single centre cam and pushrod valves, so it was pretty dull, and in this tune produced 85bhp at 4900rpm (five more than the 411) and a more impressive 109lb ft of torque at 2800rpm. The six was the 2-litre 911T engine, pure and simple – with a pair of triple choke Webers, 125bhp at 5800rpm and 131lb ft of torque at 4200rpm – in the more generous SAE figures at least. In that the 914s weighed some 240lb (109kg) less than a 911, the 914/6 might have proved embarrassingly quicker than a 911T save for the fact that the 911's simultaneously received 2.2-litre engines.

Porsche unveiled the 914 at the Frankfurt Show, late in 1969, and billed it as 'The Sports Car with the Race Car Design', just in case anyone had missed the point of the mid-engine layout. The four-cylinder was due on sale almost immediately, the six was promised for early 1970, and the prices *were* very attractive, particularly in America, where most could be expected to go. Or at least very attractive for the four-cylinder version; around $3500 was quoted for the 914, but close to $6000 for the 914/6, which put it uncomfort-

ably within sight of the 911T.

That was a reflection of political problems which had overtaken the project. Soon after entering the original and somewhat loose agreement with Porsche, VW boss Nordhoff had retired, due to ill health. He had been replaced in 1967 by Kurt Lotz, who was rather less of a friend of the family. In April 1969, anticipating the 914 launch, Porsche and VW had formalised their previously quite informal marketing arrangements by entering a fifty-fifty partnership in a joint sales company capitalised at DM5 million – purely to cover distribution. The manufacturing plan should have remained the same; VW versions of the car would be built entirely by Karmann, and the coachbuilder would supply bodies to Porsche for the six-cylinder treatment. To Nordhoff that had meant bare shells at a bare-bones price; to Lotz it meant fully-trimmed shells which were going to cost Porsche *more* per unit than a 911's. Lotz had perhaps realised that however well it sold, the little sports car was going to be very small beer in the overall VW picture and he was looking for whatever profit he could find.

Still, the four-cylinder cars sold well for a while, if never in the 30,000 a year range once anticipated; the expensive six-cylinders, on the other hand, bombed. 914/6 sales ended in 1972 with only 3360 cars made. In 1974 Porsche bought out VW's stake in the distribution company and the 100,000th 914 was sold, but the model was only struggling along. The next generation of VW management, under Rudolf Leiding from late 1971, was already looking to a water-cooled, front-engined sports car, and 914 production finally petered out early in 1976 after a total of 118,976 cars. A potentially exciting, purely Porsche, 916 version – with a 190bhp 2.4-litre 911 engine, big wheels and body to match – was stillborn after around twenty prototypes had been built, and that was the end of the mid-engined flirtation.

914, 914/6
SPECIFICATION

ENGINE
Flat-six, air-cooled

CAPACITY
1991cc

BORE x STROKE
80.0 × 66.0mm

COMPRESSION RATIO
8.6:1

POWER
110bhp

VALVE GEAR
Single overhead camshaft per cylinder bank

FUEL SYSTEM
Two triple-choke downdraught Weber 40IDT PI carburettors

TRANSMISSION
Five-speed manual (four-speed Sportmatic optional)

FRONT SUSPENSION
Independent, by MacPherson struts, lower wishbones, longitudinal torsion bars, telescopic dampers

REAR SUSPENSION
Independent, by semi-trailing arms, coil springs and auxiliary rubber springs, telescopic dampers

BRAKES
All discs, ventilated fronts

WHEELS
Bolt-on, steel discs (light-alloy discs optional)

WEIGHT
2110lb (957kg)

MAXIMUM SPEED
c.125mph (200kph)

NUMBER MADE, DATES
3350, 1969–72

911
CARRERA RS 2.7

It was almost nine years from the time of its 1963 introduction before Porsche put the hallowed name 'Carrera' onto a 911, and that was over seven years after it had last appeared on the ultimate 356 Carrera 2. In those days, Porsche treated the name with a real reverence, and although it had occasionally graced racing models like the 904 and 906 in between times, it was a big step to append it once again to a derivative of one of the mainstream roadgoing production cars.

Fortunately, few would dispute that the car in question was worthy of the name, which Porsche suggest was bestowed only on models offering 'outstanding performance and appearance'. The 911 Carrera RS 2.7 offered both, and it had a specific racing role ahead of it too. That would prove to be the foundation for over a decade of top-level racing success for

911 derivatives, including an outright Le Mans win in 1979 for Kremer's K3 version of the Group 5 935 – the last time when a recognisably production-related car, however extremely modified, won the classic event.

The Carrera RS was built as a homologation car, in this case intended to qualify for the prevailing Group 4 modified production sports car category of the FIA's world championships. That required a minimum production of 500 cars, which was a difficult number for almost any manufacturer – far too small to justify a start-from-scratch design-and-production approach, considerably too large to mean that the whole production run would ever actually be raced, or to mean that price was no object to a large majority of potential customers. As such, it all but guaranteed that eligible cars

The return of one of the great model names; when Porsche re-created the Carrera, they weren't afraid to shout about it (left). Not every spoiler from every manufacturer since has been so honest, but the RS's 'duck-tail' (overleaf) had a truly functional role.

What could be simpler, more handsome or more enduring than the elegant rear window line of the 911 (below)?

would be uprated versions of existing series production models, road usable for the majority of customers who wouldn't want to race; and in that respect Porsche had a brilliant starting point in the 'ordinary' 911.

The first Carrera RS 2.7s appeared late in 1972. At that time, the standard production capacity for the 911 was 2.4 litres, arrived at by lengthening the stroke of the 2.2-litre engine late in 1971. That increase had been aimed as much at meeting new US emissions requirements as at increasing power per se; but even with lower compression ratios, peak outputs had been increased by a worthwhile amount, to as much as 190bhp for the 911S. That made for the quickest 911 to date, but for racing Porsche still needed rather more.

Specifically, they would like an engine displacing more than 2.5 litres but less than 3 to qualify them for that division. Initially. 2.7 litres was as far as they could go without an even bigger redesign. They achieved that by increasing the 2.4's bore yet again, from 84 to 90mm, while leaving the stroke unchanged, at 70.4mm – and even to achieve that bore size they had to resort to linerless, Nikasil-coated cylinders, which coincidentally gave a useful reduction in friction. Other changes were minimal; compression was left standard at 8.5:1 and the Bosch mechanical injection was as on the 911S, so the power increase was fairly modest – to 210bhp at 6300rpm and 188lb ft of torque at 5100rpm.

But that was only part of the Carrera RS's rationale. The other racing essential is to 'add lightness', and although the RS started with the standard shape of the 911S, its weight was pared right back. Wherever possible, compatible with body strength, it used thinner gauge steel for the main shell; the engine cover was moulded in glassfibre, window glass was

thinner, and there was little or no sound or heat insulation; the rear seats were dispensed with altogether, and the front seats were replaced by much lighter, thinly upholstered racing buckets; in fact anything that didn't have to be there *wasn't* there.

For customers who really did propose to go racing, there was the lightest version of all, which Porsche labelled RSR. These were stripped to the bone and had further lightweight panels such as aluminium door skins and bonnet lid. Porsche quote a weight of 2285lb (1037kg) for the road car, 2115lb (960kg) for a production lightweight, and as little as 1985lb (900kg) for an RSR.

In familiar fashion, Porsche had been as conservative as ever about production numbers. Group 4 required 500, but in total they built 1580 RS 2.7s in 1973, which also qualified the bulk of the cars for the less rarefied Group 3 category. Of those 1580, 1331 were in a slightly more conventional 'touring' trim, and not much different inside from a standard 911S; another 200 were the 'lightweight roadgoing model', with minimal trim but not the most extreme body lightening options; and the remaining forty-nine, known as the RSR, were in off-the-shelf Group 4 trim, stripped of all fripperies and with even more power on offer. For the 1973 effort in the World Championship for Makes, that involved a further small capacity increase, to 2.8 litres, and enough other modification (including twin-plug heads, stronger crankcase, and far more extreme cams) to give first 300bhp and eventually as much as 330 when capacity reached virtually the full 3 litres.

The lightweight roadgoing Carrera RS 2.7 was the fastest production car in Germany when it was launched, with a top speed of 150mph (240kph) and the ability to reach 60mph in

The rear rim widths were increased for the RS, and the wheelarches were subtly flared to accommodate them (above), with the rear bumper and skirt neatly following suit. The engine cover was in glassfibre.

Part of the lightening process was to throw away all the superfluous trim, including the rear seats, and to replace the front seats with superbly shaped lightweight 'buckets' (right). Five-speed gearbox was standard RS wear.

The five-spoke alloy wheels were colour-coded to the Carrera script, and all in arrestingly bright colours (left), while the deeper front air-dam gave front-end downforce to balance the rear duck-tail – and was soon reflected in equipment for lesser 911 models.

around the five second region – a leading-edge supercar yardstick even today, almost twenty years on. A full-race RSR might improve those figures to over 170mph (273kph) and less than four seconds.

Obviously, Porsche had changed many other things from the standard 911S to cope with such performance. Most obvious was that the production RSs sat on noticeably wider wheels, in the distinctive and attractive five-spoke pattern. At the back, rim width was up to seven inches (for traction as well as for cornering power), although the fronts stayed at the usual six inches. The five-speed gearbox was always specified as standard, where lesser 911s still offered only four speeds as standard for most markets; springing was stiffer and Bilstein gas dampers were used, together with thicker roll bars; with the lighter weight, the ventilated but non-assisted disc brakes gave an RS stopping power that was every bit as impressive as the performance.

And Porsche didn't hide the Carrera RS's light under a bushel. The rear arches had to be widened to accommodate the bigger rear wheels, and there was a neat but unmissable graphics kit, which painted the wheel centres in primary colours and blazed a matching 'Carrera' script along the lower flanks, in a broken stripe which was repeated in the front and rear bumpers-cum-airdams. Then there was the 'ducktail' – the distinctive rear spoiler which sprouted from the engine cover and apparently reduced rear-end lift by almost 200lb (90kg) at maximum speed. It helped improve both cornering grip and straightline stability, not just by the downforce but by moving the centre of aerodynamic pressure back by a few inches. Compared to the massive fixed wings of later Turbos, for instance, the 'ducktail' looks almost subtle now, but in 1973 it was a sensation and naturally it gave the car an instant nickname.

It was a car way before its time in roadgoing performance terms, and for acceleration in particular few cars since have matched its almost violent intensity and response. So much of what followed on progressively more powerful road cars stemmed from the RS, and so much of the next decade's racing success, that it is almost certainly the most pivotal 911 of them all.

911 CARRERA RS 2.7
SPECIFICATION

ENGINE
Flat-six, air-cooled

CAPACITY
2687cc

BORE x STROKE
90.0 x 70.4mm

COMPRESSION RATIO
8.5:1

POWER
210bhp

VALVE GEAR
Single overhead camshaft per cylinder bank

FUEL SYSTEM
Bosch mechanical injections

TRANSMISSION
Five-speed manual

FRONT SUSPENSION
Independent, by MacPherson struts, lower wishbones, longitudinal torsion bars, telescopic dampers, anti-roll bar

REAR SUSPENSION
Independent, by semi-trailing arms, transverse torsion bars, telescopic dampers, anti-roll bar

BRAKES
All ventilated discs

WHEELS
Bolt-on, light-alloy

WEIGHT
2115lb (960kg) (lightweight version)

MAXIMUM SPEED
c.150mph (240kph)

NUMBER MADE, DATES
1580, 1972–3 (see text for breakdown)

924

A number of things, in retrospect, are surprising about the 924. The first perhaps is that it happened at all; the next is that for a car created from such an amazing variety of far from exotic parts-bin components it was as good as it was; and the third was that, against all odds, it was so successful, right up to the time when the 944 (which grew out of the 924 anyway) overtook it.

It was third time lucky for Porsche's low-price, high-volume efforts, and on the face of it it looked even less promising than the others, the 912 and the 914. The 912 had at least had clear 911 connections, and the 914 and 914/6 had been both fashionably mid-engined and nothing if not distinctive. The 924, on the other hand, apparently had nothing whatsoever to do with traditional Porsche wisdom, what with a water-cooled engine in the front and remarkably anonymous styling; in fact in the first place it wasn't supposed to be a Porsche at all, nor even a VW.

The plan for a third stab at the volume market dated back to early 1970, when it was already clear to Porsche's increasingly unpredictable partner VW that the 914 and 914/6 weren't going to set the world alight; and equally important, that with

new water-cooled VW mainstream models coming up, they might do well to divest themselves even more fully of any lingering Beetle connotations – as in the 914's air-cooled flat-four engine.

In the late 1960s, Porsche had worked on a Beetle successor with a water-cooled flat-four, mid-mounted under the rear seat, and in that project (EA266) they had seen a possible platform for a low-cost sports car; but when VW rejected EA266 in favour of what became the Golf, that was no longer a possibility. And soon, VW under Rudolf Leiding and later Toni Schmücker didn't particularly see the need for a VW-badged sports car of any kind any more (a stance which would be handily reinforced by the energy crisis of 1973); that eventually led to the break-up of the marketing partnership with Porsche and the end of the 914.

In the meantime, VW *had* seen a niche for a sports car in the increasingly sporty range from Audi, a company they had bought and revived as a marque name in the mid-1960s. So, in 1970, Leiding had commissioned Porsche to do a mix-and-match job from the Audi and VW parts bins and build a sporting Audi. It had to be a 2 + 2 coupé, with at least as much

The fatter alloy wheels of the Turbo gave the 924 (right) some of the image that had been lacking in the basic car, and turbocharging gave it much more impressive performance. As launched in 1975, the 924's slippery shape (overleaf) set new standards for low drag, and the Turbo took performance to 140mph levels.

The tail end of the 924 (left) didn't quite achieve the simplicity of the 911, but that was part of the penalty of cutting costs via the parts-bin, and the hatchback was useful.

space as in a 911, and it had to be comfortable and easy to drive for the masses.

Packaging dictated a front engine, politics dictated a water-cooled one, and that was Porsche's starting point. Having quickly settled on a 2-litre four-cylinder Audi engine, with belt-driven overhead-cam and fuel injection, they had open options on a transmission layout, including front-drive, which could have been borrowed from the new Audi 100. But before any decision was taken, VW pulled the plug completely and cancelled the project.

That hurt Porsche. Their work was well advanced and they had done reasonably well out of the design fees, but nothing like so well as they hoped to do out of some form of joint production; and once again they had apparently lost the option of a shared platform. Their reaction was rather brave; they negotiated with VW to buy back the project in its entirety, reportedly for a sum of DM160 million, which wasn't unadjacent to their design fees; they would continue to use VW and Audi components and have the new car (now unconditionally badged as a Porsche) built in the Audi factory at Neckarsulm, just north of Stuttgart.

First, though, they had to finish designing it. In part, the outstanding decisions were eased by the fact that what would become the 924 was evolving alongside another new Porsche, the much more exotic 928, and it would do the lesser model (which would appear first) no harm at all to bask in the image of big brother. So it grew up around an elegant layout of front-engine and rear-transaxle, linked by a rigid torque tube to give near perfect weight distribution; it was clothed in a shell styled in-house by Dutchman Harm Lagaay, and intended at least to evoke the feeling of big-brother 928. It looked a little bland, but in the more aggressively wheelarched and be-spoilered 924 Carrera and the derivative 944 it looked more purposefully Porsche, so maybe it wasn't too far wide of the mark.

As for the underpinnings, Porsche had plundered the VW and Audi inventory with consummate skill. Sceptics sneered that the engine was also used in VW's LT van, but for Porsche's purpose it lacked very little except perhaps a strong character – it was certainly willing, and once Porsche had added their own aluminium cylinder head and the Bosch injection it gave 125bhp at 5800rpm and 121lb ft of torque at 3500rpm. The clutch was on the engine but the gearbox and final drive were in unit at the back of the car, with a light propshaft running at engine speed through a rigid 'torque tube' linking the two ends. Porsche also used the torque tube to mount the gear linkage, giving a much better change than most rear gearbox layouts offered, and helping to damp vibrations. A four-speed manual 'box was originally specified, with the option of a three-speed Audi automatic, but a five-speed manual was optional from the end of 1977 and soon became standard.

MacPherson strut suspension was lifted from the latest Beetle for the front, plus lower A-arms from the new Golf; for the back the Beetle provided semi-trailing arms, with Porsche's transverse torsion-bars. Anti-roll bars were available, as were alloy wheels – but only as extras, to keep the price as low as possible. The brakes were solid discs at the front, with Audi

Interior of the 924 (top) was steadily improved but never completely lost the 'bitza' feel, even when the 924 had become a lot more expensive. With turbo-charging, power output of the four-cylinder engine (above) leapt immediately to 170bhp – with a bit more to come. The lattice-style wheels (left) were an attractive option for the 924 – at extra cost, of course.

Even with the Turbo's chunkier wheels, the 924 kept the smooth, slightly weak flanks of the normal 924 (far left), the bigger-arched look only appearing on the more extreme Carrera GT. One of the few major criticisms of the 924 was that the steering wheel sat a touch too low (left).

calipers, and drums at the back, courtesy of VW, who also provided the Golf steering rack and many smaller items of switchgear and trim.

Not everyone liked the looks, but the 924 was very slippery – in fact at 0.36 it was standard-setting when it was launched, right at the end of 1975. It was simply trimmed, down to a price, but comfortable – and quite a practical 2 + 2 if the +2 were tolerant children. The engine lacked refinement but wasn't short of performance, so the 924 was good for around 125mph (200kph) and 0–60mph in 10½ seconds. Best of all was the handling; with virtually fifty-fifty weight distribution and carefully detailed suspension, it was exceptional, with a combination of high limits, superb balance and a forgiving nature – although the ride and road noise were initially almost as bad as the handling was good.

It wasn't nearly as cheap as it might have been, it *was* basic and unrefined in many ways, and its character was atypical of a Porsche, but it found its niche and within a few years it was accounting for around 60 per cent of Porsche sales. And it was continuously improved and uprated, in both trim and mechanical specifications, albeit growing ever more expensive.

The harsh ride was tackled in 1977 with suspension changes and more insulation, alloy wheels and five-speeds became standard by 1979, equipment levels were significantly improved in 1981, and there were occasional limited editions such as 1980's 100-off Le Mans celebration, with special paint and a spoiler.

More fundamentally, a 170bhp, 140mph (225kph) Turbo version was launched in 1978, with suspension and brakes to match, in a stiffer, be-spoilered shell, sitting on bigger wheels. In 1980, Turbo power went up to 177bhp, but even that wasn't the most potent of the production 924s. That appeared in 1979 as the 210bhp, 150mph (240kph) 924 Carrera GT, which had a much more aggressive look thanks to wider wheels covered by much wider arches, and also had heavily uprated suspension, transmission and brakes.

Spoilers and air-ducts aside, it looked very much like the 944 which was about to follow. That model gave the 924 a detuned version of its all-Porsche 2.5-litre four-cylinder engine in 1985, to create the 924S, but it also started to steal the 924's sales, and come 1988 the 924 was retired – honourably.

924
SPECIFICATION

ENGINE
In-line four-cylinder, water-cooled

CAPACITY
1984cc

BORE x STROKE
86.5 × 84.4mm

COMPRESSION RATIO
9.3:1

POWER
125bhp

VALVE GEAR
Single overhead camshaft

FUEL SYSTEM
Bosch K-Jetronic injection

TRANSMISSION
Four-speed manual

FRONT SUSPENSION
Independent, by MacPherson struts, lower wishbones, coil springs, telescopic dampers (anti-roll bar optional)

REAR SUSPENSION
Independent, by semi-trailing arms, torsion bars, telescopic dampers (anti-roll bar optional)

BRAKES
Discs front, drums rear

WHEELS
Bolt-on, steel discs (light-alloy optional)

WEIGHT
2260lb (1025kg)

MAXIMUM SPEED
c.125mph (200kph)

NUMBER MADE, DATES
150,951, 1976–85

935
COUPÉ

From time to time, the rule-makers like to remind us of the relationship between race cars and road cars, especially in the sports car discipline. The all-new Group 5 which defined the World Championship for Makes from 1976 was one such occasion, when eligible cars had to be recognisably derived from production models, both mechanically and visually, and with strictly controlled modifications. In fact to be eligible for Group 5 at all, a car had first to have been homologated for one of the lesser Groups, 1 to 4, which in turn imposed minimum production requirements. Group 5 didn't demand any further 'production' run, and allowed a good deal of additional modification, but it made at least a token gesture towards limiting the extremes.

It did so by setting limits for minimum weight and maximum tyre width (both related to capacity); it restricted the size of add-on aerodynamics, and required that a number of basic components be retained from the homologated model – including many major engine components, the suspension layout (if not detail design), the engine position, and the majority of the body shell.

Within that framework, with the 930 as a starting point and the RSR Turbo for race experience, Porsche managed to create a car which anyone could see was based on a 911, but which produced as much as 850bhp in its most extreme forms, and had a top speed close to 220mph (353kph). Resuming Porsche's winning ways in the Makes series in 1976 (after a five-year lull), it continued to dominate in private hands into the 1980s, and even scored a remarkable, outright Le Mans win in 1979, for the Kremer team.

It certainly wasn't a road car, but it still stands as the ultimate, recognisable development of the 911 line. It was called, quite simply, the 935.

Somewhere under all the aerodynamic addenda that kept it on the ground and the sponsorship messages that kept it on the championship trail, the 935 coupé (left and overleaf) retained the unmistakable 911 shape.

Contrary to appearances, Group 5 regulations limited the size of aerodynamic devices such as the high rear wing and downforce-producing wheelarches (below), but the signwriting emphasised them anyway.

The production 930 (or 911 Turbo, previewed in Paris in October 1974 and closely related to the RSR Turbo), had been planned specifically as the homologation base for the forthcoming Group 4, and thence Group 5 – and as such it had initially been thought of as a 400-off limited series. Having taken a break from racing in 1975 to develop the 930 into the 934 for Group 4 and the 935 for Group 5, Porsche had already done much work on transforming it from hugely rapid but highly civilised road car to pukka racer, even before the FIA announced the minimum weight limits for 1976. For the 935 (which would nominally be a 4-litre car once its actual capacity of 2856cc had been multiplied by the turbo 'equivalency' factor of 1.4), the pertinent minimum was set at 970kg – and so successful had Porsche been in their weight saving that they had to ballast the car by some 70kg to comply.

They had removed everything surplus to racing requirements, and that included every scrap of insulation and rust-proofing, all trim, and every seat bar the driver's, which sat on a titanium base. The windscreen and driver's side window were in glass, but everything else was replaced by lightweight Perspex. The door skins, bonnet and engine cover and huge new wheelarches were all in glassfibre. And in practice, having to put ballast back on the car wasn't a total loss, because Porsche could at least position it to promote optimum weight distribution.

After much circuit testing, they put most of it as far forward as it would go in the nose (shades of early 911 lead-loaded bumpers!) and the rest near the front of the cockpit floor. Heavy items like the battery, fire extinguisher, and oil and fuel tanks also went into the nose, to balance the rear engine.

That was also based on the 911 Turbo unit, if heavily modified. As required, the crankcase, cylinder barrels and crankshaft were essentially standard (with permissible modifi-

cations), while almost everything else was extensively revised, including an uprated lubrication system and horizontal rather than vertical cooling fan. Although they used standard valves, the air-cooled heads had much improved porting and full-race camshafts, and the inlet and exhaust manifolding was new. Bosch mechanical injection was used, with the nozzles situated in the manifolds.

To arrive at 2856cc and keep the 935 within the 4-litre class, Porsche left the stroke as on the standard 3-litre but reduced the bore by a couple of millimetres. Originally, a single large turbo was used, but interpretation of the rules landed Porsche in trouble with the layout. On the first 935, they put an air-cooled intercooler in the big aluminium and plastic rear spoiler, but the FIA objected and Porsche were forced to compromise (at an awkward stage in the season) with smaller, water-cooled intercoolers and all the heavy, complex plumbing that that implied.

Nonetheless, the 935 started with almost 600bhp and 440lb ft of torque, which meant a four-speed gearbox was perfectly adequate – again derived from the very strong unit introduced in the 930 with just this application in mind. The job of stopping it all was handled by huge ventilated and cross-drilled discs and four-pot calipers, all derived from the mighty 917 racer. Suspension retained most of the production layout but changed the torsion bars for ultra-light titanium coil springs, and gave the driver cockpit control of the anti-roll-bar settings.

Between intercooler arguments and occasional mechanical failures, the 935 had a mixed debut year in 1976, but at the end of it had won the World Championship for Makes. It had also swapped the normal 911 headlamp layout for the distinctive flat-nose style, with lights in the deep front airdam and the multiple slots above the wheels adding front downforce.

Stripped to basics, the single-seat cockpit (above) was still recognisably 911-derived. Angled rev-counter sets the red-line at the vertical, in common racing practice; boost gauge is very prominent and although there is no speedometer, there is the facility to adjust roll-stiffness. The car shown here is the 935 'Baby', an even lighter version of the group 5 car with a 370bhp 1.4-litre flat-six turbo engine, built specially for the two litre division of the German sports car series in 1977.

Putting the intercooler into the rear wing on the first 935s landed Porsche in trouble, and the later wing (left) was only there to keep the car on the ground – and to carry the all-important sponsor's message, as with the nose (above) and doors (left, below).

For 1977, the only real opposition for the 935 came from other 935s, as Porsche began to sell customer cars, while they increasingly concentrated on winning Le Mans outright with the Group 6 936. A twin-turbo development for the 935 had also given another 40bhp or so, and better throttle response, and that engine was soon made available to the customer teams, it being no surprise at all when the 935 won the Makes title again in 1977.

But although the 935s had been dominant, Porsche had to accept that the 911-based six was now perilously close to its absolute limits – not so much in the bottom end, which remained robust and reliable, as in the cylinder heads and especially the gaskets, which had given all sorts of trouble during 1977. Still, it could have been worse; Group 5 required the 'block' to be standard but allowed modifications to the heads, and Porsche took advantage of that in 1978 with the most extreme of all 935 engines – in an equally extreme car which was soon nicknamed 'Moby Dick'.

They added four-cam, four-valve heads with water-cooling – the first time they had ever used it beyond the test bench. They forsook the 4-litre limit by taking the engine to 3210cc and a nominal capacity of 4495cc, which meant minimum weight increased to 1025kg. On went the ballast again, but in that the 935/78 gave 845bhp, it wasn't a problem. Clever interpretation of another rule change also allowed Porsche to lower the whole centre section of the car, and with exaggeratedly long nose and tail and all that power it would reach well over 220mph. It raced only twice, winning at Silverstone but managing no better than eighth at Le Mans, handicapped by excessive fuel consumption.

That was the works' last outing with a 935, but far from the end of its career. Private cars continued to win the Makes title right up to 1981, when the 956 appeared, and at Le Mans in 1979 the 935 had its finest hour. As the rather poor Group 6 entry (including two works 936s) faltered, the hordes of 935s moved in for the kill. At the end, it was the Kremer car driven by Klaus Ludwig and brothers Don and Bill Whittington which won, followed by another 935 driven by Rolf Stommelen, Dick Barbour and actor Paul Newman. Another 935 was third and a 934 was fourth. The Kremer 935 K3 had numerous small developments specific to the team, but none of them took away the unmistakable 911 look. Le Mans is unlikely to see such a result again.

935 COUPÉ SPECIFICATION

ENGINE
Flat-six, air-cooled

CAPACITY
2857cc (3999cc with 1.4 × turbo equivalency formula)

BORE × STROKE
92.8 × 70.4mm

COMPRESSION RATIO
6.5:1

POWER
590bhp

VALVE GEAR
Single overhead camshaft per cylinder bank

FUEL SYSTEM
Bosch mechanical injection, two KKK turbochargers

TRANSMISSION
Four-speed manual

FRONT SUSPENSION
Independent, by MacPherson struts, lower wishbones, coil springs, telescopic dampers, anti-roll bar

REAR SUSPENSION
Independent, by semi-trailing arms, coil springs, telescopic dampers, driver-adjustable anti-roll bar

BRAKES
All ventilated discs, with adjustable front/rear balance

WHEELS
Centre-lock, light-alloy

WEIGHT
2138lb (970kg)

MAXIMUM SPEED
212mph (340kph)

NUMBER MADE, DATES
Two works cars, 1976; 13 similar customer cars, 1977

911
TURBO (930)

By the early 1970s, the 911 had become an outstanding sports car; in 1974 it became a supercar, in the guise of the 911 Turbo (or more properly, the 930). At a stroke, power leapt to 260bhp, top speed to more than 155mph (250kph) and the 0–60mph yardstick came down to less than six seconds. The roadgoing Turbo would not have been out of place on a big-league race circuit only a couple of years before; and, of course, racing was the bottom line.

Like the four-cam Carrera engine, the Turbo was the inspiration of Professor Ernst Fuhrmann, the engineer who had emerged from the design office in 1972 to run the restructured company. And the Turbo was as fine an example as you might wish of racing lessons being carried over for the road, something which Porsche had learned to do better than any other manufacturer.

So, although Porsche weren't actually the first to offer turbocharging on a road car (or even on a racer), they were certainly about to become the most glamorous.

Turbocharging is one form of supercharging – feeding air to the engine under pressure, to help it burn more fuel and produce more power. A conventional supercharger is driven mechanically from the engine and thus absorbs some power; a turbocharger is driven by normally wasted exhaust gas energy, with virtually no power penalty. It does have drawbacks in that the extreme temperatures of exhaust gas (particularly in a petrol engine) demand special materials for the turbine, and the very high speeds at which the compressor must run demand very efficient bearings; sophisticated applications like racing cars and road cars need careful control of the pressure generated; and because the spinning turbo has some inertia, there can be a short delay in throttle response ('turbo-lag') – but the pay-off is in potentially huge power gains.

The principle isn't new; it was patented as long ago as 1905, and by the late 1950s it was quite common on diesel truck engines – which didn't have such an exhaust temperature problem, weren't too worried about a compact installation, and didn't particularly need instant throttle response. Better materials and design had created more compact and durable units by the mid-1960s, and US oval-circuit cars, mainly running on methanol fuels, adopted them for racing, in a discipline where near-constant maximum power was all-important, not part-throttle flexibility.

A cliché if ever there was one, but never truer than with the original 911 Turbo – this view (right) was the only one that any other car normally saw. The visual changes (overleaf) from any 'ordinary' 911 were no more than any hot-rodder might have done but the effect was spectacularly aggressive.

Porsche were far from reticent in emphasising the 911 Turbo's competition connections, either in the exaggerated body bulges and heavy-duty aerodynamic add-ons, or in the sponsor's colours (left) as used on some limited edition cars.

It wasn't so much the Indy cars that inspired Porsche, though, as something closer to home. In 1969, BMW tried turbocharging the 2002 saloon racer, and the fairly basic set-up worked well enough to give the car a lot of extra power and a few wins before the authorities banned it from production racing. Soon after, Porsche started looking at turbocharging for their racing cars, mainly for Can-Am, where they had retrenched with the mighty 917 pending changes in sports car rules in Europe. By turbocharging the 917's flat-12, Porsche unleashed the most power then seen from a racing engine – well over 1000bhp in 5.4-litre form, and quite enough to dominate Can-Am until the rules were changed again . . .

Meanwhile, back in Europe, two things were happening. A new, production-based World Championship of Makes was taking shape for 1976, as Group 5; and as early as 1972 BMW were planning to put the 2002 Turbo on the road as a production model. The first of those gave Porsche the incentive to homologate a turbocharged version of the 911 on which to base a heavily modified Group 5 car (the 935); and the second gave them the impetus to sell it as a production car, to stay ahead of their German rivals, whose next step looked certain to be a turbocharged sports car.

In 1973, Porsche tested a 2.7-litre turbo version of the 911, as a road, car. It drew on Can-Am experience and had some familiar problems, notably the troublesome turbo lag, but making things work is Porsche's forte. At the Paris Show in September 1973, the wide-wheeled Turbo with its huge rear wing was a dramatic centrepiece on the Porsche stand. It wasn't a production model yet, but it was going to be, because to qualify for Group 5 Porsche had first to homologate a 'production' model in a lesser Group – in this case Group 4, which required a minimum run of 400 cars.

The Paris Show car was actually a non-running mock-up, but the technology was coming along. In 1974, Porsche produced the first turbocharged 911 racer, a version of the Carrera RSR which they could modify to their heart's content so long as they only ran it as a prototype. As such it was allowed a capacity of 2142cc, which when multiplied by the notional 'equivalency' factor for turbo engines kept it just within the 3-litre prototype limit. With a single KKK turbo it gave 500bhp or more in qualifying trim and it was a successful test bed for what was to follow. Alongside it, the road car to achieve the homologation was evolving against the background of the Arab–Israeli war, the attendant fuel crisis, and a general downgrading of image for fast, expensive and highly consumptive cars. BMW even delayed the 2002 Turbo, but Fuhrmann stood his ground and the 930 survived.

More than that, it emerged at the 1974 Paris Show as a highly priced, luxuriously equipped, ultra-high performance model which had resisted all temptations to compromise. Engine size was up to 3 litres, mainly to improve low-speed 'off-boost' throttle response, and although the dimensions were as on the Carrera, the engine was largely new, and hugely strong. With a single KKK turbo, Bosch K-Jetronic injection, and electronic ignition, it produced 260bhp with a peak boost of 0.8bar. The power spread was kept as wide and progressive as possible, to help drivability, and the chassis was heavily upgraded to the same ends.

Visually not much more spectacular than any other hidden-from-view 911 engine installation, but the flat-six engine (above) with single turbocharger was hugely more powerful from the start – and grew even more so. The massive rear wing (left) helped with both downforce and cooling.

By restricting their clever cosmetic surgery on the 911 to the voluptuous wheel-arches and below-the-belt-line spoilers, Porsche avoided the need to change expensive items like the rear light lenses (left).

Turbo power and torque required only four gears on the floor, but demanded some big numbers on the dashboard (left) and a good deal more rubber between it and the road (left, below).

A new and massively strong four-speed gearbox was specified, with a stronger clutch. Suspension geometry was revised all round, to suit much wider wheels and tyres, and the rear hubs and suspension arms were made a lot more robust. Brakes were the ventilated RS Carrera type, and in fact only just about up to the task because the fastest 911 to date was also the heaviest. Finally there was the look, with the huge arches and the big rear wing; it couldn't help but succeed.

Production proper started in 1975 and in true Porsche tradition never looked back, the notional 400 sales proving no problem whatsoever, even though luxury equipment levels meant a luxury price. And naturally, the Turbo was acclaimed as the fastest and finest 911 to date by anyone who drove it.

The original was merely a starting point. In 1978, Porsche went a stage further, increasing capacity to 3.3 litres and power to a nice, round 300bhp. It was a case of more of everything; stroke was lengthened and the bores widened, an air-to-air intercooler was added to make the turbo even more effective, the bearings were bigger and the compression ratio was higher. On the chassis side, the brakes were updated to keep pace with the added power – adopting cross-drilled discs with four-pot calipers, inherited from 917 racers via the 935.

As much as anything, those changes were aimed at making the car even more drivable while keeping pace with tougher legislation, and they did so admirably, leaving the Turbo with only one more major revision to come over the next decade. Torque had been improved slightly and fuel consumption dramatically for 1983, but the last big change came in 1986 when a bigger turbo and intercooler plus a new exhaust system helped to increase the power again, to 330bhp, the top speed to over 170mph (273kph) and take the 0–60 time down to just over five seconds. In that guise, the Turbo survived until 1989, and just for once in Porsche history, not everyone thought its successor was an improvement . . .

911 TURBO (930)
SPECIFICATION

ENGINE
Flat-six, air-cooled

CAPACITY
3299cc

BORE x STROKE
97.0 x 74.4mm

COMPRESSION RATIO
7.0:1

POWER
300bhp

VALVE GEAR
Single overhead camshaft per cylinder bank

FUEL SYSTEM
Bosch K-Jetronic injection, single KKK turbocharger

TRANSMISSION
Four-speed manual

FRONT SUSPENSION
Independent, by MacPherson struts, lower wishbones, longitudinal torsion bars, telescopic dampers, anti-roll bar

REAR SUSPENSION
Independent, by semi-trailing arms, transverse torsion bars, telescopic dampers, anti-roll bar

BRAKES
All ventilated discs

WHEELS
Bolt-on, light-alloy

WEIGHT
2940lb (1335kg)

MAXIMUM SPEED
c.160mph (257kph)

NUMBER MADE, DATES
22,542, 1978–89

MODERATORE CAROLO DESERTAM
SOLITUDINEM LABOR IMPROBUS
QUADRIENNIO VICIT
MDCCLXIII— MDCCLXVII

928S

Die-hards, even today, might say that the only real Porsches have horizontally-opposed, air-cooled engines slung behind the rear wheels, à la 356 and 911. Porsche themselves have never been so dogmatic. By the early 1970s, development chief Helmuth Bott had already outlined a number of reasons why Porsche might soon build a car with a front-mounted, water-cooled engine. In particular, he suggested several areas where such a layout might offer improvements over the Porsche 'norm' – from better noise suppression and emissions control, through improved handling balance and accident protection, to increased passenger space and more effective heater systems. Herr Bott, for one, had seen that there was scope for more than one type of Porsche.

His report coincided with changes at Porsche. The company itself was restructured, with the Porsches and Piëchs taking more of a supervisory role and delegating direct control. There was new management of VW too, and by 1971 they had scrapped Porsche's well advanced work on the intended Beetle replacement, in favour of what became the Golf. Thus, Porsche (for a while at least) lost the promise of a low-cost, high-volume, mid-engined, joint venture with which to re-place the only partly successful 914/6 and plug the gap below the 911. Against that background they started to look to the other end of the market, at an even more refined and expensive car, in line with Herr Bott's proposals.

The go-ahead for an all-new Porsche was given in October 1971 by new managing director Dr Ernst Fuhrmann – on his birthday. The board looked at several options, including a large mid-engined car, but that was rejected mainly on the grounds that it would be difficult to provide adequate occasional seats or proper luggage space; and, as Porsche were learning to their cost even with the modest 914, that hurt sales. Nor would they build a full four-seater, because Porsche built sports cars not saloons, and they have a popular in-house saying that translates as 'cobbler, stick to your last'; or, do what you do best.

So Project 928 would be a two-door GT, with front-mounted, water-cooled V8 and rear-mounted gearbox (with manual or auto options) for optimum weight distribution. Although not quite a true four-seater, it would have reasonable 2+2 ability and it would be the biggest car that Porsche had yet built.

Some fourteen years before the 968 (in background in picture, left) was launched, the 928 (foreground in same picture) set a new, softer family style, carried through in this 928S. The big front-engined car (overleaf) had a different sort of presence from a 911.

The moulded side-strakes (below) first appeared on the 928S, to break up the visually over-heavy slab sides of the original, but little else had changed in the softly moulded lines.

A wheelbase of 98.5 inches (2500mm) (some 9 inches longer than a 911's) was set, plus figures for overall length, width and height. The basic premise of front engine and rear gearbox, joined by a torque tube, was agreed and development proper started in November 1971. At that stage a short-stroke V8 of almost exactly 5 litres and with a target of 300bhp was envisaged. Single cams and hydraulic tappets would give acceptable cost and easy maintenance but with good refinement. The chassis was expected to use some variety of wishbone suspension all round.

The torque tube layout was also destined for a smaller front-engined car (which would become the 924), but it gave problems. Without a gearbox between flywheel and prop-shaft, the long shaft turned at engine speed (not at the much lower gearbox output speed as it would in a 'normal' layout) and gave both noise and vibration problems. The original design with the clutch in unit with the rear transaxle, plus a shaft with a centre bearing, was abandoned in favour of a clutch on the flywheel and a stronger propshaft with bearings only at its ends. Further noise and vibration damping were achieved by mounting components such as the gear lever and the battery box on the drivetrain, and by mid-1973 the basics needed only detail finishing.

Meanwhile, engine, transaxle and chassis problems were being worked through. Fundamentally, the engine had to be as light and as shallow as possible (the latter to allow a low and slippery nose) and it had to be clean, efficient and light on maintenance requirements. The first example ran in January 1973, but only until the block cracked; a redesigned unit ran in March and broke again; the third version (with injection, as planned for production) gave the engineers what they wanted.

Transmission and chassis components were developed on a number of test-rig cars, variously based on or pretending to be Audis, Opels or Mercedes. A choice of five-speed manual or three-speed Daimler-Benz automatic 'boxes was finalised, and late in 1973 an almost complete 928 platform was built into a widened Audi coupé shell for testing, including desert endurance runs in Algeria.

But then, barely two years after the project had started, it was almost abandoned, as the Arab–Israeli war brought the threat of an 'energy crisis'. Porsche sales were hit overall, and the idea of an even bigger, thirstier sports car suddenly seemed embarrassingly profligate. The 928 programme was put into low gear, and the production go-ahead delayed pending improved circumstances, but ultimately Porsche bit the bullet. In November 1974, they scrapped contingency plans for either four-seater or 911-engined 928 hybrids and the original intentions were confirmed, albeit conceding a reduction in capacity from 5 to 4½ litres, and an inevitable drop in power.

On the plus side, problems with various rear suspension layouts (including torsion bar types) had been overcome with the advent of a superb new multi-link, coil-sprung rear axle. It used tiny degrees of controlled geometry change to minimise potentially troublesome lift-off oversteer, while still allowing acceptably flexible (and comfortable) bushing. Porsche called it the Weissach axle, after their R&D centre which had developed it.

The softly rounded body was also styled in-house, by a team led by Tony Lapine. With its integral bumpers clad in

Everything, but everything, about the 928's shape was designed to please the eye and cheat the wind – everything from the flip-up front lights and recessed rear lights and their moulded bumpers (top, left and right) to the smooth pillars and mirrors (above).

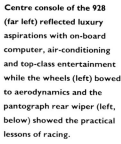

Centre console of the 928 (far left) reflected luxury aspirations with on-board computer, air-conditioning and top-class entertainment while the wheels (left) bowed to aerodynamics and the pantograph rear wiper (left, below) showed the practical lessons of racing.

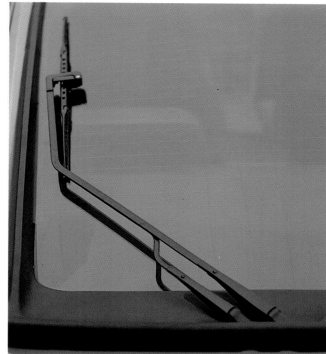

928S
SPECIFICATION

ENGINE
90° V8, water-cooled

CAPACITY
4644cc

BORE x STROKE
97.0 x 78.9mm

COMPRESSION RATIO
10.0:1

POWER
300bhp

VALVE GEAR
Single overhead camshaft per cylinder bank

FUEL SYSTEM
Bosch K-Jetronic injection

TRANSMISSION
Five-speed manual (four-speed automatic optional)

FRONT SUSPENSION
Independent, by upper wishbones, lower trailing arms, coil springs, telescopic dampers, anti-roll bar

REAR SUSPENSION
Independent, by multi-link Weissach axle, with upper transverse links, lower trailing arms, coil springs, telescopic dampers, anti-roll bar

BRAKES
All ventilated discs, ABS anti-lock system

WHEELS
Bolt-on, light-alloy

WEIGHT
3420lb (1550kg)

MAXIMUM SPEED
c.155mph (250kph)

NUMBER MADE, DATES
10,205, 1979–83

knock-absorbing polyurethane skins, plus distinctive open-style flip-up headlamps and aggressively broad-shouldered proportions, it was a car to create strong reactions. When it was launched, at the Geneva Show in March 1977, those reactions were predictably mixed. Porsche 'purists' inevitably wondered why there wasn't an air-cooled flat-six in the back, and not everyone liked the looks, but the press voted the 928 their International Car of the Year.

In fairness, there was room for criticism. The 928 was a fine Grand Tourer with an outstanding chassis, but its mid-development crisis had left it with 'only' 240bhp and it wasn't as quick as a Porsche flagship might have been expected to be. There were moans about road noise and minor details, but what disappointed most people was that the heavy 928 just wasn't quite potent enough.

In 1979, Porsche revised the standard model slightly and introduced a new version which was closer to what many people thought the 928 should have been all along; they called it the 928S. A new 4.7-litre V8 gave the full 300bhp as

originally planned, and it had better brakes to match. It was universally regarded as a huge improvement and by mid-1982 the base 928 was discontinued, while the S was further uprated with LH Jetronic injection to give 310bhp and even more performance. With a four-speed auto (rather than the original three-speed) and 'second generation' ABS braking as standard, it became the S2.

Porsche didn't use the S3 label, but there was a heavily revised S2 for the US market early in 1985, with a full 5 litres, twin-cam heads and four valves per cylinder – to maintain power while meeting US emissions needs, even with catalyst equipment. In mid-1986 that engine was adopted (with further uprating) for all markets, giving a standardised 320bhp. Styling was subtly updated with a new tail spoiler and other drag-reducing features and the car became the 928S4, with a quoted top speed of 168mph (270kph). And finally, for 1992 there will be a 5.4-litre, 340bhp newcomer with further styling updates, a top speed of over 170mph (273kph) and the label 928GTS. Like the 911, the 928 is proving very resilient.

911 Carrera 3.2

By most reasonable reckoning, the 911 should have been dead and buried by the mid-1980s, and replaced by the broad spread of the 944 and 928 ranges. But Porsche customers continued to vote with their cheque books and stubbornly refused to let the old stager die; so in 1984, instead of going quietly to the automotive graveyard, the 911 was reborn.

And this was no token gesture; far from being just another money-spinning limited edition or minor cosmetic rehash, it was something close to a full-scale updating. There was a new and more powerful flat-six, a revised gearbox, bigger brakes, and numerous suspension and body options – the latter including the elegant cabriolet style that Porsche had introduced for 1983, as well as the familiar coupés and Targas.

With hindsight, the cabriolet might be seen as early evidence that the 911 wasn't quite as near the end as some sceptics seemed to think at the start of the 1980s. Certainly it had had its problems, and the launch of the 928 in 1977 should, in theory at least, have been the final nail in its coffin; but things just don't happen that way with Porsches, and when the 250,000th example of the marque rolled off the line in June 1977, it was, of course, a 911. The car's demise didn't even materialise when Dr Fuhrmann (champion of the 928, remem-

ber) fulfilled the next stage of his plan by introducing the 944 in 1981. 928 and 944 alike were fine cars in their own right, but they weren't 911s, and the customers simply refused to cross over.

It was a highly significant point in the company's history. After the 1972 reshuffle (in which the Porsche and Piëch families had stepped aside from day-to-day control), Fuhrmann, as chairman, had worked desperately hard to impose his own philosophy – for which read the 928 and 944 families – at the expense of the 911. Ferry Porsche himself didn't necessarily follow the Fuhrmann philosophy, but the entire point of the company restructuring had been that the new management would be allowed the freedom to pursue their own ideas, and they were.

Unfortunately, though, while the new cars were being created, the old one was being uncharacteristically neglected, on the assumption that it was about to disappear anyway.

It was an unusual situation for the 911, whose development had barely stood still since the day it was launched. It had gone from 2 litres to 2.2, 2.4, 2.7 and most recently to a full 3 litres, not only to improve power, but also to help it meet tougher emissions laws, while still remaining drivable and acceptably

Far from being killed off by the 928, the 911 tightened its grip on the affections of Porsche aficionados with the long-running Carrera 3.2 (right). As 're-born', in 1984, it had more power, better handling, and styling (overleaf) that evoked the best of the Turbo look.

By the 1980s, the 'whale-tail' spoiler (left) had become something close to a 911 trademark, but it did serve a practical purpose in improving rear-end stability at the sort of speeds the 911 had become capable of.

economical. From 1974 (again prompted by new legislation) it had adopted the new, higher bumper look, but where most manufacturers simply tacked on ugly compromises for the US market, Porsche took the trouble to redesign for a world market, and the 911 looked better for it, not worse.

Equipment levels had been constantly improved too, especially in important areas like heating and ventilation, and more comfort and convenience options were offered virtually year on year. And the chassis was gradually made to behave itself and lose its worst vices, again through constant attention – from the original mild palliative of extra weight in the front bumpers, through a slightly longer wheelbase from 1968 to improve the weight distribution, to wider wheels and wider rear track, and regular updates of tyre, brake and shock absorber specification.

But by 1978, the 911 was inescapably reflecting the fact that the past few years at Weissach had been devoted largely to the 928, and that that car, not the 911, was now expected to shape Porsche's future. The 911 range had been rationalised to just two basic models, the 300bhp Turbo and the 3-litre 911SC – which was slightly less powerful than the Carrera which it replaced, but more flexible and otherwise virtually identical. And pending the arrival of the 944, and the 911's expected demise, the SC changed little over the next few years, save for yet more comfort options – and the addition of the Cabriolet during 1982.

That was the clear sign that the 911 was still fighting – and the appearance of the Gruppe B 'design study' (the nascent 959) at Frankfurt in September 1983 only confirmed it.

The change of heart had started a couple of years earlier. By the start of 1981, with the 944 a reality, Fuhrmann had retired, to be succeeded as chairman by an American, Peter Schutz; and Schutz was a 911 enthusiast through and through, with the full backing, of course, of Ferry Porsche.

The whale-tail looked dramatic from any angle (above, left) and although the louvres (left) didn't feed an intercooler as on the Turbo, they did help to keep the engine bay cool. Five-spoke wheels (above) were still a trademark.

Thus, while the 928 and 944 were given every possible help in creating their own niches, the 911 was brought back to the centre of Porsche thinking, and plans for its 'rebirth' began to take shape. The cabriolet, for instance (a full convertible rather than the familiar and popular Targa), was first seen as a design exercise at the Frankfurt Show as early as September 1981, and the show car specification also included four-wheel drive. The all-wheel drive option would have to wait for the arrival of the 959 and the Carrera 4, but the cabriolet was offered as a production model for the 1983 model year – and car makers

Laid-back lights (left) had for a long time had lenses moulded to shape, and now they could have washers too. Door mirrors (left, below) were big but neat, and electrically adjustable.

only 80 per cent new to the normally aspirated 911. It kept the latest alloy block, with bore unchanged, but adopted the 3-litre Turbo's crankshaft, with stroke increased to give a capacity of 3.2 litres. It used bigger valves, higher compression pistons, new inlet and exhaust manifolding, and Bosch digital management. Power was increased to 231bhp, and torque even more impressively, to 209lb ft – although the new engine was usefully less thirsty.

The gearbox was given its own oil-cooler, plus new ratios to match the different engine, and the brakes were uprated again. The cabriolet, naturally, was available alongside the usual coupé and Targa shapes, and customers could also specify Turbo-style bodywork – big wheels and wings included. To go with that, there was the option of the Turbo's uprated suspension and cross-drilled brakes, all of which brought the Carrera interestingly close to Turbo territory for a lot less money. So instead of being phased out, the 911 enjoyed near record sales, and continued to survive the recession (with the inevitable updates) until the Carrera 2 took over in 1988.

Ultimately, the Schutz philosophy failed Porsche in some respects, notably in his expansionist ambitions and his heavy emphasis on the American market, which accounted for some 62 per cent of Porsche sales by late 1987. That imbalance hit Porsche hard when world economies started to head downwards in the late 1980s, leaving both sales and profits badly damaged; but Schutz had also spent wisely during the good times, to create new research and manufacturing facilities, all of which would help cushion the blow via outside research contracts.

Most important of·all, Schutz was indisputably the man who saved the 911; and even in the teeth of the recession, the 911, amazingly, was the one Porsche that everyone just kept on buying. . .

don't often indulge in expensive additional tooling for a range that they know is already condemned.

Final confirmation that the 911 was very much alive and kicking came soon enough, when Porsche revived the Carrera name again, but this time for a full-production model. And although it didn't quite match up to the exclusivity of Carreras past, there were few who would dispute that it was one of the more important 911s.

It made brilliant use of what was available, and although Porsche reckoned the engine was 80 per cent new, it was really

911 CARRERA 3.2
SPECIFICATION

ENGINE
Flat-six, air-cooled

CAPACITY
3164cc

BORE x STROKE
95.0 x 74.4mm

COMPRESSION RATIO
10.3:1

POWER
231bhp

VALVE GEAR
Single overhead camshaft per cylinder bank

FUEL SYSTEM
Bosch DME management

TRANSMISSION
Five-speed manual

FRONT SUSPENSION
Independent, by MacPherson struts, lower wishbones, longitudinal torsion bars, telescopic dampers, anti-roll bar

REAR SUSPENSION
Independent, by semi-trailing arms, transverse torsion bars, telescopic dampers, anti-roll bar

BRAKES
All ventilated discs

WHEELS
Bolt-on, light-alloy

WEIGHT
2560lb (1160kg)

MAXIMUM SPEED
c.152mph (244kph)

NUMBER MADE, DATES
76,208, 1983–9

944
TURBO

With the 944 (unveiled at the Frankfurt Show in September 1981), Porsche finally caught sight of their long-time Grail – a car to sell below 911 price levels and in serious numbers, but which the world could believe in as a real Porsche. The 914/6 had been a virtual non-starter in that respect, and although the 924 had done much better in terms of both sales and popular acceptance, the customers Porsche *really* wanted still thought of it as a dressed up VW/Audi, with badges beyond its station.

Yet in many ways there was little wrong with the 924; at least nothing incurable. In basic form it had always looked bland; its tall, narrow-shouldered look was a bit weak and feeble for a proper Porsche, but the wide-wheeled, wide-arched and be-spoilered Carrera GTs had shown that a little body-kitting could go a long way towards giving the 924 a more muscular image; and the Turbo had shown that the fine chassis could handle plenty of extra power with minimum modification. On that basis, a good-looking 924 sibling, with a pedigree Porsche engine and the performance to back the looks, was a car just waiting to be created.

Porsche had known that for some time, and the only element that was missing was an engine, but that was in hand. By the time of the launch, they had been developing what

became the 944's engine for a good four years, and it would be all their own work. They had rejected a V6 or small V8 as an unwanted complication of the engine range, and instead chose quite a brave way to go: a large capacity four – initially to be normally aspirated, but with ample options for growing more powerful over the next few years.

It was an obvious decision from the point of view of packaging, because the 924 shell (which would be used virtually unchanged) was designed around an in-line four; it fitted current thinking on economy and emissions control; and it did mean they could use many of the lessons of the 928 V8. It was less attractive, however, in that such a large capacity in-line four *should* be plagued with balance and vibration problems, which could put the car back to square one so far as refinement was concerned.

But to dismiss the new four-cylinder engine as no more than half a 928 V8 would be doing it less than justice. Because the 944 had 2.5 litres in four cylinders and the 928 had nearly five litres split by eight, there were obvious points of reference (including bore sizes and spacing, and valve layout) – but in the end, few significant parts of the two engines would be interchangeable, and the four would have one necessary further sophistication, to deal with the balance problem.

By any standards, the 944 is a purposeful looking car, and a far cry from the bland 924 from which it evolved. The stubby tail (right) looks hugely better for a neat spoiler, and the wider wheels and arches (overleaf) give the car an altogether more powerful image.

The square-jawed nose of the 944 Turbo (below) is so strongly proportioned and detailed that it looks right even with the headlights popped – and that is a rare achievement for any car.

It would be Porsche's version of an old but effective solution – twin contra-rotating balancer shafts as invented by Lanchester before World War I, and currently subject to Mitsubishi patents. Porsche briefly toyed with designing their own variant, to sidestep licencing fees, but soon adopted the existing type. Two extra shafts run parallel to the crankshaft in the block, turning at twice crank speed and in opposite directions to each other. In the 944, one is just below the inlet ports and the other is low down on the opposite side of the block, both driven by a double-sided toothed belt. They do a superb job of smoothing out the inherent imbalance of four big cylinders.

Otherwise the all-aluminium engine was quite conventional, with iron-coated pistons running directly in linerless bores, a five-bearing crankshaft, and a single overhead camshaft operating two valves per cylinder. Bosch injection and digital electronic ignition allowed a high compression ratio and the engine gave 163bhp at only 5800rpm, with a very flat torque curve.

It was mounted (inclined at an angle of 30° to keep the low bonnet line) on a pair of clever, fluid-filled blocks which further isolated the shell from any remaining vibration. Wider wheels and 'arches apart (pressed in steel rather than tacked on in glassfibre as on the Carrera), the rest of the car was similar to the 924 Turbo –· with its superbly balanced torque tube layout, strut front and trailing-arm rear suspension, and ventilated disc brakes all round. The Audi five-speed manual or VW three-speed auto options were repeated from the 924. The alloy wheels were markedly wider, at 7J × 15, and although there were more optional luxuries, the interior was very similar to the 924's.

When the 944 went on sale in 1982, it was universally well received. The engine was ultra-smooth and amply powerful, and of course the chassis was as good as everyone already knew it was – better even, with mildly revised suspension settings for the new car. The 135mph (217kph) 944 had eliminated the 924's shortcomings, and as launched it was even remarkably cheap – as Porsche knew it had to be. That advantage would soon be eroded, but from the start it became the fastest selling Porsche ever.

In familiar fashion, it was improved more or less continuously in small ways and occasionally in big ones. In 1985, for example, a new dashboard was added, and Porsche finally answered a problem first noted on the 924, that the steering wheel was too low. The 944 now adopted a smaller, height-adjustable wheel.

Late in 1985 (and delayed briefly by German industrial strikes) came a major power boost, when Porsche introduced the 944 Turbo, which had once been intended to replace the 911! It used the same four-cylinder, single-cam, two-valve engine as the 944, in the same 2.5-litre capacity, but with a water-cooled KKK turbocharger and intercooler, plus appropriately lower compression ratio. For all markets, it produced 220bhp and 243lb ft of torque, now coupled with an uprated five-speed manual gearbox, without the auto option.

The Turbo had improved suspension with cast alloy arms in place of the old pressed steel ones, and new transaxle mounts. It also had a bigger, moulded plastic fuel tank and other improvements, most of which filtered down to the normally aspirated cars. In 1987, for instance, ABS braking became standard on the Turbo and optional on others, and by 1989 it was standard across the range.

Porsche have rarely been afraid to use trim that looks odd at first but which tends to grow on you – like the subtly-strong stripes in this 944 Turbo (above). And with the Turbo, they finally offered a better steering wheel position, too.

A more sophisticated engine than appearances suggest (left), with twin balancer shafts to soften the thud of four big cylinders, and a water-cooled turbocharger to liberate lots of power. Turbo badge (below, left) signified handling and stopping improvements, too.

And there was more performance to come. In mid-1986, Porsche upgraded the normally aspirated 944 engine by adding a twin-cam, four-valve head, reflecting a similar change on the 928. With better breathing and higher compression, that put peak power up to 190bhp and top speed to over 140mph (225kph), in what Porsche called the 944S. A Turbo S naturally followed, from 1988, first as a limited edition of around 1000 cars, with 250bhp and further uprated suspension, much like the Turbo Cup cars – and that specification soon transferred more or less intact to be the standard offering. By this time, the comfort equipment (which some customers had inevitably come to expect) had piled up too, with things like air conditioning, electric windows, central locking, power steering, and electric height adjustment for the driver's seat all on the list – and, it has to be said, reflected in substantially increased prices.

In 1989, Porsche took the two-valve model out to 2.7 litres, offering 165bhp and rather better torque, and they introduced a new version of the normally aspirated four-valve car, as the 944 S2. The capacity had been increased to virtually 3 litres, which really was on the limits for a four-cylinder, even with balancer shafts. In this guise, power went up to 210bhp, and the S2 shared almost all the Turbo's chassis equipment, including suspension and brakes. A 944 cabriolet was offered too, but only on the S2, which was a sign that Porsche were rationalising the range as the 944's replacement loomed. The 2.7-litre two-valve model survived for only one model year, leaving just the Turbo, and the S2 in coupé and cabriolet versions, and when, after a long and honourable career, the 944 was replaced in late 1991 by the not dissimilar 968, the Turbo option had disappeared too.

944 TURBO SPECIFICATION

ENGINE
In-line four-cylinder, water-cooled, twin balancer shafts

CAPACITY
2479cc

BORE x STROKE
100.0 × 78.9mm

COMPRESSION RATIO
8.0:1

POWER
220bhp

VALVE GEAR
Single overhead camshaft

FUEL SYSTEM
Bosch Motronic management, single KKK turbocharger

TRANSMISSION
Five-speed manual

FRONT SUSPENSION
Independent, by MacPherson struts, lower wishbones, coil springs, telescopic dampers, anti-roll bar

REAR SUSPENSION
Independent, by semi-trailing arms, transverse torsion bars, telescopic dampers, anti-roll bar

BRAKES
All ventilated discs

WHEELS
Bolt-on, light-alloy

WEIGHT
2975lb (1350kg)

MAXIMUM SPEED
c.155mph (250kph)

NUMBER MADE, DATES
18,161, 1985–91

959

The 959 may look for all the world like nothing much more than a brashly body-kitted 911, but under those basically familiar lines is *the* most technically advanced super-car to date, and one of the fastest. But in matching its near-200mph (320kph) performance with astonishingly complex and effective chassis technology (including electronically controlled four-wheel drive and driver-adjustable suspension) it also became a uniquely user-friendly package which is argu-ably still without peer.

It is a car to be savoured by a fortunate few: hugely expensive and built in strictly limited numbers, it had the original (but effectively stillborn) intention of being homolo-gated for racing and rallying – yet that too only adds to the legend.

The clue to its original rationale is in the name under which it first appeared, at the Frankfurt Show in 1983. Exactly twenty years after the 911 had been unveiled on the same stage, Porsche presented it as a 'design study', dubbed the Gruppe B. It was meant to race under the new Group B regulations, which allowed manufacturers a good deal of technical freedom so long as they were prepared to build a

minimum of 200 identical cars. That, of course, would only be possible so long as a manufacturer could sell the majority of production; and, with no likelihood of finding 200 racing customers, that meant selling versions acceptably 'civilised' into road cars, while retaining the essential competition items. Ferrari did it with the 288GTO, and Ford with the RS200, Audi with the Sport quattro; others had their own interpre-tations, but the 959 became the mightiest of them all.

The Gruppe B was clearly 911-based. It had most of the 911's central monocoque, but clothed in a low-drag body made largely in composites. Its 956-type flat-six was also 911-related, but with water-cooled, four-valve, twin-camshaft cylinder heads and twin turbochargers; and although it was in its own tubular subframe, it still sat behind the gearbox and rear axle line. As first seen, its capacity had been increased from 2.6 to 2.8 litres, but power was limited to a comparative-ly modest 400bhp, on very low boost, for drivability and durability.

That was almost the most 'ordinary' element of the Gruppe B's specification. It also boasted a six-speed gearbox, a com-plex, electronically controlled four-wheel drive system with

The four-wheel-drive, near 200mph 959 was the most extreme roadgoing Porsche of them all (opposite and overleaf), but below the aerodynamic add-ons, its relationship to the 911 is unmistakable, especially in the distinctive roof line.

The deep, square-cut tail of the 959 gave rise to a different type of tail spoiler from any previous 911's (left), in the guise of the full-width hoop. It was a novel design at the time, but like many Porsche innovations it soon spawned its share of imitators.

viscous centre coupling and driver-controllable torque-split for changing conditions, plus race-derived brakes and suspension. It was an extraordinarily ambitious project, but Porsche promised that, once development was complete, they would build the requisite 200-minimum homolgation run and then go racing and rallying with the car, tentatively from 1985.

Even for Porsche, it was a tough target, and they didn't make it. In 1984, the Gruppe B became type number 959 as development continued. As such, it gained additional cooling vents in the nose and tail, bigger wheels with tyre-deflation sensing system, and (gradually) even more ambitious engine, transmission and suspension specs, including more responsive turbos and adjustable ride-height and damping systems. Simultaneously, Porsche added some competition mileage by entering three 911s with Gruppe B features in the 1984 Paris–Dakar Rally. Their 3-litre engines were detuned to around 225bhp (for reliability even on poor quality local fuel) and they ran with simplified four-wheel drives, but that was enough for René Metge's example to win the event.

Diluting the apparent promise were problems for the 'production' 959. The sheer complexity of the four-wheel drive was making it difficult to complete, and adding the adaptable suspension had been time consuming. Even aside from the technical delays, Porsche were hit by supply problems – through strikes in the German motor industry, which hit the exotic 959 just as hard as it hit the mainstream cars. Plans to start 959 production in 1984 for homologation in 1985 were revised, initially to envisage production starting in April 1985, and at that point Porsche even announced projected prices – of around DM420,000 for the road-equipped bulk of cars or DM650,000 for the competition version (officially designated 961). It was *very* expensive.

The car was still nowhere near production-ready by the promised date, and the three '959s' entered in the 1985 Paris–Dakar didn't repeat Metge's glory of 1984; they used full 959-style bodywork (with massive ground clearance) and the six-speed gearbox, but had 230bhp Carrera-based engines and the simplified four-wheel drive once again. Two were eliminated by accidents and the third by oil-pump failure, rather reflecting the general frustrations of the project to date.

As the prospects of an early production start continued to slip away, the 959's original raison d'etre was also about to disappear, along with Group B itself. The category had been well-intentioned in bringing manufacturers into top-class competition but, especially in rallying, had backfired. By allowing a small number of each model to be 'evolved' year on year without further homologation, the rule makers had opened the door to the most extreme cars ever seen in off-road competition, frequently with 500bhp or more and with performance not far short of GP levels. They were technically magnificent, but the rallying environment made them very dangerous. In 1985 and 1986 there was a spate of major accidents and fatalities, involving both top level drivers and, even more worryingly, spectators. Come the end of 1986, Group B was abandoned, and frankly little mourned.

Porsche still hadn't even started production of the 959, but they had advanced so far and spent so much that they did go ahead, and the long-planned run started in 1987.

Providing adequate cooling was one of the major problems during the 959's evolution, and the rear wing scoops (above) channel cool air to the tightly packed engine bay (opposite, top). The ducts behind the rear wheels (opposite, bottom) are sited just aft of the twin turbo intercoolers.

If anything, the sculpted sills (left) emphasise rather than disguise the added width of the 959's composite bodywork. The magnesium wheels featured hollow spokes for a tyre-deflation warning system.

Even the compact external mirrors (above) on the 959 paid ultimate homage to aerodynamics. The interior (below, centre) would have felt familiar to any 911 owner, save for a six-speed gear change, and additional switches and instruments for variable four-wheel drive and suspension systems.

At least the problems had been solved, and the car was simply the fastest in the world, without qualification until the arrival of Ferrari's much less complex but staggeringly powerful F40 in 1988, another limited-edition which Ferrari readily admitted was designed to re-capture the 'world's fastest' crown from the 959.

As finalised for production, the 959 had a 2.85-litre flat-six with two water-cooled turbos, four cams, and four valves per cylinder in water-cooled, forged alloy heads. The rods were titanium, the valves sodium-filled and the turbos had two intercoolers and electronic control. Below 4500rpm the first turbo alone received all the exhaust gas, for performance not unlike a 930's; above that, the electronics diverted gas into the second turbo, which blew not in parallel but in series, and the power curve climbed very steeply. It peaks with 450bhp at 6500rpm and 369lb ft of torque at 5500rpm.

That is enough to give the 'Sport' version of the road car a top speed of 197mph (316kph), 0–60mph (96kph) in 3.7 seconds and 0–100mph (160kph) in 8.3 seconds – figures way out of reach of virtually any other car, but achieved with deceptive ease in the 959 thanks to the brilliance of the rest of its specification. The four-wheel drive offers driver-selectable modes for conditions from dry tarmac to ice, plus continuous automatic variation of torque-split for optimum grip, and it is extremely difficult to break traction. Similarly, the self-levelling suspension with its stiffness and ride-height selecta-bility, and the massive, ABS-equipped brakes, give roadhold-ing and braking which make all the 959's colossal performance exploitable even in what to any other supercar might be seen as marginal conditions. Add to that the luxuries of a leather-trimmed interior, with air-conditioning and limousine equip-ment levels (at least in the Comfort version, the Sport is a bit more basic), and you have a car whose blend of refinement, performance and usability might never be rivalled.

959
SPECIFICATION

ENGINE
Flat-six, air-cooled cylinders, water-cooled heads

CAPACITY
2849cc

BORE x STROKE
95.0 x 67.0mm

COMPRESSION RATIO
8.3:1

POWER
450bhp

VALVE GEAR
Two overhead camshafts per cylinder bank

FUEL SYSTEM
Bosch DME management, twin KKK turbochargers

TRANSMISSION
Six-speed manual, variable-split four-wheel drive

FRONT SUSPENSION
Independent, by double wishbones, coil springs, twin telescopic dampers, anti-roll bar

REAR SUSPENSION
Independent, by double wishbones, coil springs, twin telescopic dampers, anti-roll bar (front and rear have height and damper adjustment on some models)

BRAKES
All ventilated discs, ABS anti-lock system

WHEELS
Centre-lock, light-alloy

WEIGHT
2977lb (1350kg) (Sport version)

MAXIMUM SPEED
197mph (316kph)

NUMBER MADE, DATES
250, 1987–8

911
CARRERA 2 & 4

Not always entirely in jest, Porsche's rear-engined cars have often been described as a triumph of development over design. Almost as frequently, some of those who served their Porsche apprenticeships on the viciously tail-happy earlier models (and plenty who have never driven a Porsche at all) bemoan the fact that every improvement in handling and civility has been an attack on the unique Porsche character.

The truth of the matter is that rear-engined Porsches, and especially older ones, have traditionally had different reactions around their limits to most cars, and to the clumsy or foolish the handling can be threatening; but equally, such road manners *in extremis* are in large part what make a Porsche a Porsche.

It is a matter of design. The rear-engined layout, even when balanced by whatever weight can be loaded into the nose, *does* guarantee a higher polar moment of inertia – a 'dumbell effect' – which likes to rotate about its own central axis. Especially in the early days of swinging arm rear suspension, if progressively less so with semi-trailing arms, Porsches *have* been inherently prone to oversteer should the driver suddenly lift off the power in mid-corner, as a forward weight transfer makes the nose bite and prompts the heavy tail to try to overtake it.

Of course, many cars (including mid-engined and even front-drive ones) do the same thing, but with the rear-engined Porsche the car could occasionally beat the driver.

But look back and you will see that nothing is new under the sun. In November 1953, testing an early 356, *The Autocar* noted: 'There is pronounced oversteer, as with all rear-engined cars, and, as with a racehorse which might bolt unless a firm hand is on the reins, so one must be in control here, as it is possible to bring the tail round very quickly if the driver is too enterprising on wet surfaces.' By October 1958, driving a 356A 1600, the same magazine reckoned, 'years of development have gone far towards removing any handling shortcomings resulting from the rear-engine layout; once a driver has grown accustomed to the car, it is easily controllable on dry or wet roads, provided, of course, as with any high-performance car, that the power-weight ratio is borne in mind

The retractable tail spoiler (right) which Porsche developed for the Carrera 2 & 4 was a neat element of the cars' back-to-basics smoothness. It flips up at open road speeds and disappears neatly at town speeds, and it helps cooling as well as aerodynamics.

The styling of the latest generation Carreras (below and overleaf) harks back to the simplicity of the earliest 911s, but it is neatly updated with strong 'family' details like the integrated nose and tail mouldings which were pioneered by the 928S.

and undue liberties are not taken.'

Or in July 1965, of an early 911: 'The handling of the 911 is superb and although you are dealing with a rear-engined car with the engine located behind the back axle, this handling is very much on the neutral side, with light oversteer appearing only under very severe conditions.' By 1975: 'Despite the reputation for tail happiness established by the 911's predecessors, this car feels more inclined to go straight on at its limit.'

And finally, with the Carrera 2 in December 1989: 'The 26-year amelioration of the 911's handling deficiencies reached its apogee with the Carrera 4 which, through sheer weight of technology, crushed tail slides precipitated merely by lifting off the throttle mid-bend out of existence. That the Carrera 2 displays a similar disinclination to let go at the back is even more impressive, especially since it is paired with a sense of agility and adjustability seldom apparent in the C4. . .'

They weren't alone in branding the new Carrera 'the best 911 yet', and Porsche's philosophy of continuous development was surely never better vindicated. The new family of rear-drive Carrera 2 and four-wheel-drive Carrera 4 shared virtually everything in their chassis make-up save the additional front drivetrain of the 4. There was the same new suspension, the same new engine, and the same, smooth, beautifully understated shape, with integrated front and rear bumpers and subtle, pop-up wing.

It was still unmistakably a 911 through and through, but Porsche reckoned that it was 85 per cent new. The flat-six had grown to 3.6 litres, with redesigned crankcase, a new crank, new rods, pistons and cylinder heads. The inlet and exhaust plumbing was revised, and there were now two plugs per cylinder, with twin distributors and the latest Motronic management. With 250bhp and 210lb ft of torque, it became the most powerful normally aspirated 911 production engine to date, with almost double the power of the first, 130bhp flat-six of twenty-six years earlier.

Most notable of the suspension changes was a switch to coil springs, while keeping the essential layout of struts and lower wishbones at the front, and semi-trailing arms at the rear. For the first time, Porsche offered ABS braking, on typically huge ventilated discs all-round. And for the first time other than on the ultra-specialised 959, they offered four-wheel drive, with variable torque split.

Drive was taken forward from the gearbox to a central transfer box which gave a nominal split of 31 per cent to the front, 69 to the rear, and used a version of the 959's PSK electronically-locking clutch system to apportion torque according to demand. With another PSK in the rear axle, the system could vary torque split according to detected slip at either end – in theory sending up to 100 per cent of the drive to either end. It would react in only four hundredths of a second to speed differences between wheels, but also had a degree of 'intelligence', to differentiate real slip from other similar effects.

Additionally, the Carrera 2 offered an option that hadn't been seen on a 911 since 1979 – an automatic gearbox. The last auto option, Sportmatic, was a 'clutchless manual' change, but successful and well regarded; the new one is called Tiptronic and is a sophisticated system which gives the driver the option of fully automatic or clutchless manual changes, with 'intelligent' shift programmes. It was developed via the PDK double-clutch system on the 962C endurance racing cars, and in Tiptronic it combines a torque-converter auto with a combined manual and automatic shift system, developed jointly by Porsche, Bosch and ZF. The neat gate has a normal

The engine bay of the current 911s (above) is visually no more exciting than it has ever been, and the flat-six is now also largely encapsulated from below for better sound deadening, but with twin-plug heads and capacity up to 3.6 litres, this is the most powerful normally aspirated 911 engine of all.

The heater controls are much simplified from older models, and the centre tunnel is deeper to allow for four-wheel drive parts, but the Carrera interior (left) is basically familiar – save for the long-absent option of an automatic gearchange (left, centre). A tell-tale for this excellent Tiptronic auto appears in the speedo (left, bottom).

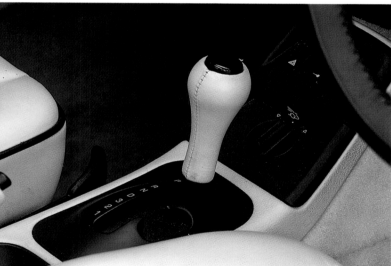

PRND32 sequence on the left, and opposite D, via a short slot, another much smaller gate on the right, marked with a plus sign forward and a minus sign back from the lever's spring-centred M (for manual) position.

In the left-hand gate, Tiptronic is a fairly conventional auto, but cleverer. It allows the driver to select manually and to hold lower gears, but its 'Intelligent Shift Programme' will override undesirable changes, for instance before or in a corner, where a normal auto might change and upset the balance of the car.

And the '+/−' gate gives the option of one-touch, clutchless 'manual' changes, almost motorcycle style – a prod forward to change up, a snick back to change down, always sequentially, of course. Changes can be made without lifting from the throttle, and so long as the ISP knows that they aren't at an inappropriate moment or won't over-rev the engine, for instance, they happen virtually instantaneously; otherwise, the ISP will remember the instruction and change when it is safe to do so; ignore the need to change up and it will do so for you without over-revving.

It is undoubtedly a brilliant and versatile system and Porsche immediately began to develop it even further, with more ratios and even more sophisticated shift programmes.

The new Carreras were almost universally reviewed as the most competent 911s ever, with great refinement and handling that had finally become almost idiot-proof, and that is where the second element of Porsche tradition began to creep in. While praising the car's new brilliance, the majority of testers also found it a little clinical. As so often before, the die-hards seemed to find it hard not to mourn the passing of the old treacheries – or what we tend to call Porsche character. Same as it ever was. . .

911 CARRERA 2 & 4 SPECIFICATION

ENGINE
Flat-six, air-cooled

CAPACITY
3600cc

BORE x STROKE
100.0 × 76.4mm

COMPRESSION RATIO
11.3:1

POWER
250bhp

VALVE GEAR
Two overhead camshafts per cylinder bank

FUEL SYSTEM
Bosch DME management

TRANSMISSION
Five-speed manual (Tiptronic automatic optional)

FRONT SUSPENSION
Independent, by MacPherson struts, lower wishbones, coil springs, telescopic dampers, anti-roll bar

REAR SUSPENSION
Independent, by semi-trailing arms, coil springs, telescopic dampers, anti-roll bar

BRAKES
All ventilated discs, ABS anti-lock system

WHEELS
Bolt-on, light-alloy

WEIGHT
3040lb (1380kg)

MAXIMUM SPEED
c.160mph (257kph)

NUMBER MADE, DATES
1989–1993

911 TURBO

By a fairly small margin, the 1991 911 Turbo became the quickest 911 ever; by a significantly larger one it became the most expensive 911 ever; and to look at the specification – combining the acknowledged brilliance of the latest Carrera 2/4 chassis with an even more powerful and flexible version of the classic turbocharged flat-six engine – it ought also to have been welcomed as the most convincing 911 of them all. But for once there were strangely unaccustomed reservations . . .

The new Turbo was launched at the Geneva Show in March 1990 with the promise of a production start by the end of the year. As such, it left a breathing space after its predecessor had gone out of production in 1989. For a while, it had seemed like the car that was never to be, a car that Porsche had once said they wouldn't build. To some, it also seemed like a car that had finally slipped out of its time, launched at a show where there was far more talk of environmental protection and corporate regrouping against recession than about outright performance and money-no-object self-indulgence.

And even if you cared to dismiss the latter as the cyclical downside of the perennial optimism/pessimism nature of things, it maybe didn't look quite different *enough* from its predecessor to generate the sort of instant excitement that the Turbo once had.

As *Autocar* observed, 'It looked like a mellow 959 with its vast flared wheelarches and five-spoke alloy wheels, but there was a general feeling that Zuffenhausen should have waited a year until releasing the Turbo. Then it would have featured the new six-speed manual gearbox and a four-valve version of the 3.6-litre Carrera 2 engine with another 50 or so bhp. In the face of supercar activity from Lamborghini and Ferrari and the coming Bugatti, Jaguar XJ220 and Mercedes C112, the Turbo is no longer the supercar standard setter . . .'

You might also argue that for any version of a near twenty-seven-year-old model even to be mentioned in the same breath as such new and vastly more expensive ultra-cars as the Diablo, the Bugatti and the Jaguar said everything about

Although it generally follows the smooth-bumpered, deep-silled look of the Carrera 2 & 4 models from which its chassis is derived, the latest Turbo (left and overleaf) also has the familiar Turbo styling themes of oversize wheel arches and the big, fixed 'picnic-table' spoiler.

The Turbo is further distinguished from its less potent siblings by the new and rather 959-like alloy wheels, and smaller, more aerodynamic door mirrors (below); there's still no mistaking the classic roof and window line, though.

The familiar rear spoiler (above) again covers the generously proportioned intercooler which sits above the engine bay (opposite, top). The cross-drilled and ventilated brakes (left) now feature **ABS** as well as the usual four-pot calipers.

people's expectations of the Turbo; and that, in the end, may have created its biggest image problem.

Mechanically, it should have had everything going for it. In its brief sabbatical, the Turbo had gained 20bhp, a catalyst-clean conscience, and the outstandingly effective 85 per cent chassis newness of the Carrera 2. The former stopped short of Porsche giving the Turbo a version of the latest twin-spark, 3.6-litre flat-six of the normally aspirated models, but the old 3.3-litre Turbo engine had received considerable attention. It had better inlet and exhaust manifolding (the latter with three-way catalyst), revised mapping for the ignition and K-Jetronic injection, a bigger KKK turbocharger and intercooler, and revised turbo wastegate – now with its own silencer and catalyst, so as not to dump unwanted back pressure into the main system or unwanted pollution into the atmosphere. It also gained the 'double-mass' flywheel from the new 3.6 engines, which improved both noise and vibration damping. The dimensions and the capacity, at 3299cc, were unchanged, but peak power improved from 300 to 320bhp and peak torque from 300 to 332lb ft respectively.

It continued to 'make do' with five speeds rather than the alluded-to six, but for long enough Turbos had managed with four, and why a fairly compact car with 332lb ft of torque might need six is perhaps a matter for conjecture.

As on the Carreras 2 and 4, the Turbo's chassis at last lost the torsion bar suspension of previous models, and adopted coil springs for its MacPherson strut/lower wishbone front and semi-trailing-arm rear. For this still quicker car, the springs, dampers, and anti-roll bars were all made a bit stiffer again, and the rear arms were beefed up to handle the combination of more power and torque with bigger tyre

footprints. The layout also now allowed a small degree of passive rear geometry change, to tame the rear-steering characteristics on lift-off.

Other additions suggested a further shift in character – not quite enough to amount to going soft, but arguably enough to imply a new theme of idiot-protection. For the first time, there was power steering, and ABS anti-lock braking on even bigger ventilated and cross-drilled brakes with four-piston calipers all round. The brakes were better cooled, too, inside larger diameter wheels with a more open five-spoke pattern; and the wheels and tyres were again larger enough than on the

provements have been made to the interior', but, details apart, few drivers of older 911s would have felt lost.

On paper, it all added up to a car that was usefully the quickest in its range, and by no means disgraced in even the most exotic of supercar company. The top speed was within a whisker of 170mph (273kph), with the ability to leap from rest to 60mph in less than five seconds, to 100mph in less than 11.5 seconds, and from 0–120mph (193kph) in something under 17 seconds – all of which would apparently suggest awesome acceleration and outstanding flexibility, but alas that was only partly true.

In everyday practice, a number of testers, author included, found the new Turbo to have developed a strange kind of split personality. Unarguably, given the benefit of wide-open spaces and the opportunity to keep the turbocharger spinning hard, it was a hugely fast performer, its power kept well in check by its superb new chassis competence and unfailingly reassuring brakes. Even the power steering detracted not at all from the sharp and informative feel of the road, and the engine retained much of the aural character that the 3.6s had rather lost.

But there was a catch. Point the Turbo away from the smooth and wide roads on which it impressed so much and it began to show chinks in its armour. Not the chinks of old, where the combination of enormous power and old-generation suspension might snap at the unwary, but more a lack of spontaneity and a worrying loss of even the cloak of refinement. In short, the bigger turbocharger, even though producing less peak boost and supposedly with a redesigned rotor for better response, had introduced an unacceptable lethargy from low engine speeds in higher gears – turbo-lag by any other name. In some circumstances it was embarrassingly bad, often needing two downchanges where once you might have been irritated to have needed one. And more annoyingly still, it compromised the expected brilliance of the new chassis, by taking away the driver's option for precise and instantaneous throttle control.

On top of that, the lower profile tyres that were the corollary of the larger diameter wheels, and the stiffer springing, introduced a degree of harshness to the ride, and a level of road noise on poor surfaces, that even the stiffest of earlier 911s had hardly approached. It was a strange set of circumstances to have imposed itself on a car that was once so uncompromising, and maybe, just maybe, it showed up the outer limits.

normally aspirated Carreras to give the Turbo its characteristic broad haunches.

Up to a point, the new Turbo had the clean and simple lines of the other new Carreras, with the deeper but fully integrated front and rear bumpers-cum-airdams, and the neat, low sills; but it also had the wider arches, and where the others had the small rear wing (which retracted shyly below around 50mph (80kph) but popped discreetly up above that), the Turbo stuck with the old, fixed, full-sized picnic-table wing, incorporating the intercooler.

Inside, Porsche announced that 'numerous functional im-

The interior and dashboard layout of the latest Turbo (left, below) might be rather more luxurious and elaborate than those of the earliest 911s, but they are recognisably related. One thing that has changed is the numbers, and a 180mph speedometer (left) is not fanciful for a 170mph car.

911 TURBO SPECIFICATION

ENGINE
Flat-six, air-cooled

CAPACITY
3299cc

BORE x STROKE
97.0 x 74.0mm

COMPRESSION RATIO
7.0:1

POWER
320bhp

VALVE GEAR
Single overhead camshaft per cylinder bank

FUEL SYSTEM
Bosch K-Jetronic injection, single KKK turbocharger

TRANSMISSION
Five-speed manual

FRONT SUSPENSION
Independent, by MacPherson struts, lower wishbones, coil springs, telescopic dampers, anti-roll bar

REAR SUSPENSION
Independent, by semi-trailing arms, coil springs, telescopic dampers, anti-roll bar

BRAKES
All ventilated discs, ABS anti-lock system

WHEELS
Bolt-on, light-alloy

WEIGHT
3218lb (1460kg)

MAXIMUM SPEED
c.170mph (273kph)

NUMBER MADE, DATES
1991, 4107

911
CARRERA RS

On the face of things, the 1991 Carrera RS might look like a giant leap backwards in modern Porsche philosophy – a car which started with all the refinements of the latest generation Carrera 2 and then apparently threw most of them out of the window, in a return to raw basics; but that, paradoxically, is what must guarantee its future reputation as one of the great ones.

Simply in carrying the RS badge it had a lot to live up to, and in their own press material Porsche themselves headlined the September 1990 debut of the new car with the words 'Rebirth of a Legend'. The legend they alluded to, of course, was the ducktailed 911 Carrera RS 2.7 and 3.0 cars of the early 1970s; and the new RS, which went into limited production in 1991, was the first Porsche to carry those initials since then. In Porsche-speak, the letters are 'exclusively reserved for a lighter and more powerful version of a given model'; which is precisely what the 1991 Carrera RS is.

That 1973 RS was launched to homologate the 911 for Group 4 Special GT racing, and it was the start of a line of racing 911 derivatives, up to and including the turbocharged 935 coupés, which dominated Group 5 in the late 1970s just as

comprehensively as the RS, RSR and RSR Turbo had dominated their own categories in the middle of the decade. The 1970s RS gave rise to a family of racing models, the 1990s RS evolved out of one.

It was based on the cars raced in the 911 Carrera 2 Cup series, a one-model racing championship launched in Europe in 1990, for Carreras with strictly limited modifications. Those modifications weren't aimed at increasing outright speed so much as at enhancing circuit drivability and safety, and promoting as competitive a match of cars as possible. In essence they amounted to a small increase in power, a marked decrease in weight, and appropriately revised suspension and brakes. And what Porsche saw as good for the Carrera Cup racers, they saw as being good, too, for the sort of roadgoing Carrera 2 driver who would put up with rather less comfort and refinement for rather more excitement – a commodity which die-hard 911 enthusiasts had suggested was less apparent in the Carrera 2 than in its ancestors.

So, as with the Cup cars, the starting point for the roadgoing RS was the Carrera 2, and the sports-orientated reasoning that says less adds up to more. It meant farewell to

The smooth-nosed body styling of the new **RS** (overleaf) is essentially identical to the normal **Carrera 2 & 4** models, but the lowered ride-height in particular gives a more aggressive look. The more aerodynamic wing mirrors (right) are borrowed from the latest 911 Turbo.

It took Porsche a long time to put the **RS** script (left) back on the engine cover of a Carrera; the initials stand for *Renn Sport*, and this production model was based on the Carrera 2 as modified for the one-model Carrera Cup race series.

Carrera 2 comfort options like the electric windows, electric mirror and seat adjustment, central locking, power steering, the alarm system, the sunroof, and air conditioning. The rear seats were jettisoned too, along with much of the more civilised mainstream car's sound deadening under-trim, leaving just a carpeted shelf in the back of the cockpit, which was more useful for luggage than for even the hardiest of passengers. And anyway, access to the back was seriously curtailed in the RS because the normal front seats were replaced by solid-shelled racing buckets, which don't even have back-rake adjustment but which do provide the most positive and comfortable location for a hard-charging driver.

The Carrera 2's fully trimmed door panels were substituted by the simplest of flat mouldings, with no oddment pockets, manual window winders, and simple nylon loops for the door pulls. And don't even think about looking for a radio or a cassette player, because, of course, there wasn't one.

That added up to a claimed weight saving of maybe 10 per cent over a standard Carrera 2, which equates to around 280lb (127kg), bringing the overall weight down from some 2980lb to just over 2700lb (1230kg). The 'more' side of the equation started with the familiar, all-aluminium, air-cooled, flat-six, which in this case was almost identical to that of the Carrera 2. That meant a capacity of 3.6 litres, from the very oversquare bore and stroke dimensions of 100.0×76.4mm, twin overhead camshafts per bank and twin plugs, but still only two valves per cylinder. For the RS it retained a version of the Carrera 2's Bosch DME electronic engine management, and

even the environmentally friendly catalyst exhaust, but modest changes to the management mapping gave small increases in maximum power and torque, plus maximum responsiveness and flexibility.

In terms of numbers, it meant a jump from 250bhp to 260bhp, at an unchanged 6100rpm, and from 228 to 240lb ft of torque at 4800rpm. Combined with the weight saving, it lifted the RS's power to weight ratio from the Carrera 2's 188bhp per ton to a highly respectable 216, and that gain alone was enough to change the whole feel of the car.

It was only part of the story, though. An even bigger change of character came from what Porsche did to the chassis, and all of that was aimed principally at those who would use their RS on the race track – whatever the consequence for real-road manners.

Starting at road level, the RS sits wider and lower. The five-spoke magnesium-alloy wheels are similar to those used on the Cup model, 17 inches (430mm) in diameter and with front and rear widths of 7.5 and 9 inches (190 and 228mm) respectively; they were chosen to allow the car a possible role in Group N/GT production sports car racing, where tyre choice is free but rim size has to be as standard – and Porsche planned to have produced the necessary 1000 examples of the RS for Group N/GT homologation by the end of 1991, on the way to a projected total run of approximately 2000 cars. Usual factory tyre choice was the Yokohama A008P, which was official wear for the German Porsche Club racing series, and also normal fitment on the Turbo. It was a fine tyre for circuit

The wheels (above, left) are Turbo style, with the rim size fixed by racing needs and the open pattern giving better cooling for uprated brakes. The flat-six (top) is only mildly modified, but its character changes markedly. The RS motif is repeated on the steering wheel (above) but the driver should not need reminding.

Porsche resisted any temptation to fit the big, fixed Turbo-style rear wing to the RS and settled for the neat retractable spoiler from the Carrera 2 & 4. With the spoiler down (right), the RS's tail is as uncluttered as on any 1960s 911 model.

Minimalism was the order of the day for the RS interior (left), with the simplest of trim, deletion of almost all the electrically operated options like windows, seats and mirrors, and even the radio. The racing style seats are flamboyantly trimmed but offer quite superb location at speed.

use, with an asymmetrical tread pattern and an ultra low profile (in 205/50 and 255/40ZR17 front and rear sizes for the RS) but it was also the starting point for a much harsher and less forgiving chassis feel for an RS on any less than perfect road surface.

The Carrera's ride-height was also lowered by 40mm (about 1.6 inches) and both springs and dampers were made markedly stiffer. The front brakes were the bigger, ventilated, cross-drilled discs from the Turbo, the rears were taken from the Carrera Cup cars – and even compared to the already excellent brakes on the standard Carrera 2, they gave astonishing stopping power and feel, further emphasising the RS's character as a racer which could be used on the road rather than as a road car which could go racing.

The change in look was subtle, principally noticeable in the more aggressive wheel and tyre spec and the minimal ride height – with no additional spoilers beyond the neat pop-up rear wing of the Carrera 2 to break the pure 911 line. Inside, the car felt purposeful, especially in the deep-sided, wing-shouldered racing seats and the almost complete lack of trim – not quite spartan, but certainly no more than functional. But dynamically it felt like an old-style 911 reborn.

Gone was any of the understatement of the Carrera 2, and back came all the glorious immediacy of the most exciting 911s of all. On the road, the low and stiffly sprung RS could leap and dart about in nightmare fashion on broken surfaces or awkward cambers, but on anything fast and smooth, and especially, of course, on the tarmac ribbon of a race track, it became the epitome of 911 motoring. Claimed maximum speed was unchanged, at 160mph (257kph), and Porsche say the 0–62mph (0–99kph) acceleration time had only fallen from 5.7 to 5.3 seconds, but the feel of the car bore little relation to the figures. Far from the muted civility of the Carrera engine installation, the RS had the chilling rawness of the best of older 911s. It had instantaneous and exceptionally precise throttle response, matched by a superbly slick gearchange, razor-sharp steering and those astounding brakes. The dulling understeer of the Carrera 2 and even the Turbo was replaced by a superbly neutral and roll-free stance that made it a car crying out to be driven on its limits, and that's what makes it wholly worthy of a badge which Porsche have never used lightly, and never more so than today.

911 CARRERA RS SPECIFICATION

ENGINE
Flat-six, air-cooled

CAPACITY
3600cc

BORE x STROKE
100.0 × 76.4mm

COMPRESSION RATIO
11.3:1

POWER
260bhp

VALVE GEAR
Single overhead camshaft per cylinder bank

FUEL SYSTEM
Bosch Motronic management

TRANSMISSION
Five-speed manual

FRONT SUSPENSION
Independent, by MacPherson struts, lower wishbones, coil springs, telescopic dampers, anti-roll bar

REAR SUSPENSION
Independent, by semi-trailing arms, coil springs, telescopic dampers, anti-roll bar

BRAKES
All ventilated discs, ABS anti-lock system

WHEELS
Bolt-on, light-alloy

WEIGHT
2634lb (1195kg)

MAXIMUM SPEED
c.160mph (257kph)

NUMBER MADE, DATES
2364

968

For many years after its 1982 launch, Porsche did very nicely with the 944. In its heyday, when the car was relatively inexpensive and when the world economy was in better shape, the front-engined four-cylinder range achieved peak annual sales of well over 20,000 units, or comfortably over half Porsche's total output; it built a reputation for having one of the most competent, user-friendly sporting chassis in the world; and it rarely stood still for long – developing from the original 163bhp 2.5-litre model through the 190bhp 16-valve S to the 211bhp 3-litre 16-valve S2 and the 250bhp Turbo, latterly available in both coupé and handsomely sleek cabriolet options.

It had the knack of staying fresh, but it also had a stigma; it never *quite* managed to distance itself as far as Porsche would have liked from the 'bigger-engined-924' image, and it never quite rose above the nagging thought that it was assembled by Audi, not by Porsche themselves. In many ways, especially in the more potent later versions, it was one of the most practical and accomplished cars Porsche made, but somehow it also

contrived to move even more relentlessly away from its entry-level pricing than it had from its entry-level image, until sales were going backwards. By the end of the 1980s, it was time for the 944 either to move on or move over.

Of course, Porsche considered the first alternative very carefully, looking at how they might have broadened the existing 944 coupé/cabrio range, with, perhaps, a 'high-performance-estate' version, a Speedster in the mould of the low-'screened 356 and 911 variants, a cabrio-shaped hardtop, or, naturally, performance-oriented upgrades – from a moderately quicker GT to a savagely powerful hybrid using the 928's then-5-litre V8.

In the worsening economic climate, though, the danger was that, however unjustly, any simple range-expander might still carry the 944's image problems, and Porsche would prefer something more.

And so the go-ahead was given in 1989 to produce not a sister but a successor, available just in the familiar coupé and cabrio shapes and with the new label, 968. When they

Like its predecessor the 944, the '80 per cent new' 968 offers a handsome and versatile cabriolet version, which look equally good with the double-lined and electrically operated hood either down (opposite), or up (overleaf).

The proportions of the 968 cabriolet, with its deep body sides and relatively low top, and especially its steeply raked windscreen (left), give the car a look not unlike that of a classic mid-1950s Speedster.

introduced it, in the summer of 1991, Porsche avowed that it was '80 per cent new', and that it would be built not by Audi at Neckarsulm but by Porsche at Zuffenhausen, alongside the 911 and the 928; and if those of a more cynical disposition tended at first to think of it as a new number on a basically old car, they were at least generous enough to admit that much *had* changed.

Most obviously, the rebirth started with the looks. Cover up the nose and tail and you'd be in no doubt as to the 968's 944 parentage, but look at the whole car and you will see shades of 928, and even Carrera 2/4 – all underlining that insistence that the 968 is all Porsche and all grown up. The nose, in particular, is strikingly handsome, a cross between the pure smoothness of the 928 and the classic raised-wing look of the 911, with perhaps more than a hint of 959. The tail is 944 above and including the simple spoiler, and a neater, more stylishly integrated update of 944 below, with much simpler tail-lamp clusters under single-colour wrap around lenses, and a smooth-moulded bumper line without the odd lip-spoiler that used to hang under it. The flanks were unchanged except for the sills, which more closely resembled those on the Carrera 2, plus body coloured door handles and Turbo-style door mirrors. The cabriolet's roofline was left as low and swoopy as ever, and the 968 arguably looks best of all in soft-top guise with the roof erected, but at the expense of a rather claustrophobic feel inside that would be familiar to any mid-1950s Speedster driver. . .

As well as making the 968 look different from the 944, the new body shape made it a bit more slippery and also made the crumple zones even more effective. It still isn't the most aerodynamic sports car in the world, but Cd figures of 0.34 for the coupé and a surprisingly similar 0.35 for the cabriolet

The biggest changes between the looks of the 944 and those of the 968 are in the even smoother nose and tail treatments (above and above left), which manage to give a family affinity with the 928 while still looking very individual. The laid-back headlight theme has survived into the 1990s, and body-coloured door handles (left) are another neat touch.

As well as looking good (left), the latest style of Porsche five-spoke alloy wheel, much as on the Turbo and RS 911s, offer more internal space for bigger brakes and more ventilation for better brake cooling.

are reasonably respectable, and Porsche also reckoned that the new shape creates less high-speed lift at the tail.

New wheels helped change the look of the car, too – neat five-spoke alloys, similar in pattern to those on the Carrera Cup 911s, the Turbo and the Carrera RS. And as well as just looking good, their more open pattern allowed better brake cooling.

Under the skin, the basic building blocks – the big, counterbalanced four-cylinder thumper of an engine, the 944 floorpan, centre sections rooflines and interiors, and the 944's highly regarded transaxle and suspension layout – were essentially carried over, but most parts changed to greater or lesser degrees.

There is no longer a Turbo option as there was in the 944 range, largely because Porsche couldn't afford to finance two development programmes in one, and because they believed that the large capacity, naturally aspirated engine offered virtually all the benefits with few of the hassles. So the big bore four-cylinder engine with twin-shaft counterbalancing appeared in the 968 in the same 3-litre, 16-valve guise as in the 944 S2, but with some technically interesting and very effective updating.

Most fundamental was a new variable inlet-valve timing system, which Porsche dubbed Variocam. It is neatly integrated into the camshaft chain tensioner and controlled by the Bosch Motronic engine management system. At low engine speeds it adopts the basic, quite mild timing for smooth low-speed running with minimum emissions; at higher speeds, it will advance the opening of the inlet cam by up to 15°, thereby increasing the overlap between inlet and exhaust valve opening and improving torque delivery; beyond the point where torque is less important, from about 5000rpm, it eases back to

the normal setting again to deliver maximum power.

Complementing that were improved inlet manifolds with resonance effect, new inlet valves, more efficient exhaust plumbing with a less restrictive catalyst and big-bore pipework, lighter pistons and forged con-rods, and revised management. The gains were significant; peak power improved from 211bhp at 5800rpm to 240bhp at 6200rpm (only 10bhp short of the supposedly less responsive Turbo), and peak torque rose from the S2's 203lb ft to 221lb ft, although it didn't arrive any earlier than the original's rather high 4100rpm. As before, a 3-litre four-cylinder engine, even with twin balancer shafts, has to be on the ragged edge of refinement, but there's no mistaking that its pulling power is better than that of any other normally aspirated 3-litre.

Porsche now hooked it up to either a new six-speed manual gearbox or a version of the Tiptronic automatic, still with four speeds but in this case with even more features than that introduced in the Carrera 2 – notably even more capacity to analyse driving style and modify shift patterns accordingly.

The power-assisted steering and ABS-equipped brakes came directly from the latest 944s, and the suspension kept the 944's layout but with revised settings, while Porsche also now offered a Sport option, with adjustable dampers and spring height, still more stiffness, 17-inch-diameter wheels (430mm) and bigger brakes.

Most drivers reckoned the 968 was pretty sporty already, probably even improving on the hugely respected 944 in every respect except engine refinement and cabin ergonomics, which was one of the things that Porsche, surprisingly, had done little or nothing to change. It would be considerably more expensive, and it is unlikely ever to sell in the sort of numbers that the 944 achieved at peak, but it's a real Porsche.

968
SPECIFICATION

ENGINE
In-line four-cylinder, water-cooled, twin balancer shafts

CAPACITY
2990cc

BORE x STROKE
104.0 x 88.0mm

COMPRESSION RATIO
11.0:1

POWER
240bhp

VALVE GEAR
Two overhead camshafts, four valves per cylinder

FUEL SYSTEM
Bosch Motronic multi-point injection

TRANSMISSION
Six-speed manual (Tiptronic automatic optional)

FRONT SUSPENSION
Independent, by MacPherson struts, lower wishbones, coil springs, telescopic dampers, anti-roll bar

REAR SUSPENSION
Independent, by semi-trailing arms, transverse torsion bars, telescopic dampers, anti-roll bar

BRAKES
All ventilated discs, ABS anti-lock system

WHEELS
Bolt-on, light-alloy

WEIGHT
3020lb (1370kg)

MAXIMUM SPEED
c.155mph (250kph)

NUMBER MADE, DATES
May 92–1995, 11245

911 CARRERA
(Type 993)

Times were hard for Porsche in the early 1990s, and it was only the timeless rear-engined 911 which retained its popularity. Careful juggling of models, engine tunes, and specifications kept it in the limelight. Front-engined Porsches, on the other hand, died away.

Long-awaited new models were cancelled, and even the American market seemed to be tiring of the immortal 911. The 968 - an extensive revamp of the popular 944 - was a total failure. For a time, it seemed, only Porsche's prestigious consultancy activity kept the business afloat.

It was deep-breath time. Management took a number of far reaching decisions, and laid down an aggressive master plan for the late 1990s and beyond. Not only would they start to develop a series of completely new cars, but there was time for one last major update of the air-cooled 911 theme.

Apart from retaining the basic layout of the well-loved 911 – an air-cooled flat-six engine in the extreme tail, two-plus-two seating in coupé or open-top guise, a low nose and long, sweeping tail – almost every other aspect of the car would be changed, this time for an assembly-line

life of just four seasons. Although the design philosophy of the revised 911 was rooted in the 1960s, 30 years later the execution was very different.

Working under project code '993', the engineers not only developed a very different chassis/platform, but the stylists reworked the basic shape, making this the most rounded and arguably the most appealing 911 so far. If only we had known it, the new shape, which was unveiled in 1993, was also an introduction to what would be adopted for a further all-new 911 in 1997.

Although the 993 looked rather like the 911s which had gone before, there were many changes, all intended to soften the car's appeal. The cabin, and the basic proportions were retained, but laid-back, ellipsoid Bosch headlamp lenses were a new feature, as were the flowing and integrated lines of the front and rear bumpers. The wheel tracks were wider, and so were the wheel-arch flares, though the interior of the cabin itself was little changed.

Technically, though, the secret of reviving the 30-year-old chassis was hidden away. After only four years, the platform of the existing 911 (which had itself been much changed

Although the design philosophy of the revised 911 was rooted in the 1960s, 30 years later the execution can be seen to be very different.

in 1989) was revamped yet again. Up front, there was the same type of MacPherson strut front suspension, but at the rear there was a new type of aluminium double wishbone/coil spring rear suspension, this being the very first of the road cars to discard VW-inspired torsion bars.

Although the overall weight distribution was little changed (63 per cent was still over the driven rear wheels), Porsche claimed that the chassis changes had considerably tamed the over-steering tendencies of earlier models. The engineers, in fact, had been very busy. Not only was the twin-cam-per-bank flat-six engine pushed out to 3.6-litres, where it developed an understressed 272bhp, but it was now matched by a new six-speed all-synchromesh gearbox. A clutchless Tiptronic S switchable manual/automatic alternative was also to be available during 1994.

Wider wheel tracks, sharper steering, new front suspension geometry, larger brakes and the latest Bosch ABS antilock layout all added up to a great chassis, reborn. This car, in fact, was only the first of a new (but short-lived) family of 911s. A four-wheel-drive version was soon on the market (the Carrera 4), a phenomenally powerful, 408bhp, four-wheel-drive Turbo version was also planned, as were limited-production versions which would include a light-weight 300bhp Carrera S.

By the time assembly ran out in 1997, a Porsche customer for these 911s needed a brochure, and a session in a quiet corner to make his choice, for there were two- or four-wheel-drive types, manual or Tiptronic transmission, coupés, Targa-tops, and full drop-top cabriolets, all built

with Porsche's usual attention to detail, reliability, and high-speed refinement. At Stuttgart-Zuffenhausen, Porsche production, which had fallen to a mere 12,000 cars in 1993, rose sharply to more than 23,000 in 1996, of which 20,765 were 911s – a sure sign of the latest 911's popularity.

By most other makers' standards, 272bhp was phenomenally powerful, but to Porsche in the 1990s, this was straightforward stuff, and although the engine (complete with a high, 11.3:1 compression ratio) was obliged to run on 98 Octane Unleaded, it was amazingly flexible.

Britain's *Autocar & Motor* magazine said it was 'the sharpest and friendliest 911 yet, and because you can drive

Apart from retaining the basic layout of the well-loved 911 – an air-cooled flat-six engine in the extreme tail, two-plus-two seating in coupé or open-top guise, a low nose and long, sweeping tail – almost every other aspect of the car was changed.

it harder and indulge yourself yourself more deeply, the rewards remain both delicious and attainable.' The revised chassis delivered all its promise: final oversteer was still present, but not to a vicious degree, for this was an extremely controllable layout. Weissach insiders, on a confidential basis for months previously had been saying the same sort of thing: 'It's like the old car, only better. Much better. It's more explosive down the straight, handles more crisply, rides more comfortably, steers more precisely, and stops more strongly.'

Although the new car was heavier than the old, it also had a larger capacity, and an engine with more torque, so its performance, and its character, could still astonish. On the one hand it was a truly accomplished *autobahn* stormer, on the other a refined town carriage. Neither the engine, or the ultra-wide tyres made it quiet, but it was certainly more refined and more flexible than any equivalent Ferrari.

Straight-line performance, as expected, was stimulating. Because of the engine-over-driven-wheels layout, there was no change of getting it away from rest with a shriek of wheelspin, but 60mph was attainable in 5.2 seconds, 100mph in a mere 13.2 seconds, and within half a minute of total acceleration, a new 911 owner could be cruising an unrestricted German *autobahn* at around 140mph.

The top speed was up to 170mph if conditions were right - but this was only part of the latest 911's appeal. Fifth gear, at a stirring 6,800 engine rpm, was good for 142mph, fourth for 119mph, and even third could deliver 94mph.

Yet here was a car which pulled like a horse from 20mph in fourth gear, or no more than 40mph in sixth - what more could any sports car lover want ?

The short answer, sometimes, was more sophistication - but within the same model range Porsche could deliver all that. If they were to improve on this machine, with a new-generation of 911s, their renowned engineering team would have to work more miracles.

911 CARRERA (TYPE 993)
SPECIFICATION

ENGINE
Flat 6

CAPACITY
3600cc

BORE X STROKE
100 × 76.4mm

COMPRESSION RATIO
11.3:1

POWER
272bhp

VALVE GEAR
Double overhead camshafts, four valves per cylinder

FUEL SYSTEM
Bosch Motronic engine management, and fuel injection

TRANSMISSION
Six-speed manual

FRONT SUSPENSION
Independent, by MacPherson strut, coil springs, anti-roll bar, telescopic dampers

REAR SUSPENSION
Independent, by double wishbones, coil springs, anti-roll bar telescopic dampers

BRAKES
All discs

WHEELS
Five-bolt alloy

WEIGHT
3021lb (1370kg)

MAXIMUM SPEED
168mph (270kph)

YEARS IN PRODUCTION
1993 – 1997

BOXSTER

After years of false starts, of deep introspection, and of financial trauma, Porsche finally launched the first of a totally new generation of cars in 1996. Called the 'Boxster' it was not only different from any previous Porsche, but was also considerably smaller and cheaper than other recent products from Stuttgart.

Although it 'grew up' a lot during its development (the early concept car of 1993 was at once smaller, and simpler), the Boxster was a more affordable sports car than Porsche had been used to making since the 1970s. Although every element of the old pedigree was present, the details were new and fresh.

As an open-top two-seater – a real sports car, as opposed to a larger coupé with the top cropped off – in many ways this was a throw-back to the much-loved Speedster of the 1950s, a better, smoother, well-developed and more sensible up-date of the 914/6 theme of the 1970s. Yet it was still a Porsche, a real Porsche – technically advanced, very carefully developed, and with much familiar evidence of Porsche heritage under the skin. For the die-hard enthusiasts, its most important feature was its engine, which might have been new in every way, but was still a flat-six !

Starting once again from the beginning - for Porsche boasted correctly that they were not copying anyone else - the team had produced a radical new type of two-seater. Although it was definitely only a two-seater, and the engine was still behind the seats, the engine was ahead of the line of the rear wheels, and every element of the chassis was new.

Except for the actual engine position (which could not be ideal for service and maintenance purposes) the new Boxster, in fact, embraced everything which the pundits had been demanding for so long. Compared with the long-running 911s (which were about to be replaced in any case) here was a much smaller and lighter car.

Although still recognisably shaped by the same experienced team ('You can see Porsche DNA everywhere...' was one wise comment) it reversed the old tendency to spread, to put on weight, and to put on cost. For the first time in years, here was a cheaper Porsche, and one which more people would be able to afford.

The new car, coded '986' in Porsche engineering-speak, first took shape in 1992, in a two-new-model programme, where the entire front end/sheet metal/front suspension

Although recognisably still shaped by the same experienced team, the Boxster reversed the old tendency to spread, to put on weight, and to put on cost.

For the first time in years, here was a cheaper Porsche, and one which more people would be able to afford.

was to be shared with the next generation '996' 911. Even though that car would have its engine behind the line of the rear wheels, Porsche still managed 36 per cent total commonality between the two cars.

The new unit-construction steel hull – like its predecessors it was galvanised and intended for long life – ran on a compact 95in (2,415mm) wheelbase, and placed a new water-cooled (yes, that's right, water-cooled) flat-six ahead of the rear wheels. With two seats but no provision for '+ 2' accommodation, the car had a vast front windscreen (which was also shared with the next-generation 911), coil spring/strut independent suspension all round, and a choice of a five-speed manual or an automatic transmission. The relatively small 204bhp/2,480cc engine size, or the positively lithe unladen weight of a mere 2,756lb (1,250kg) was expected. For sure, it was still going to be a fast car, but by previous 911 standards a 139mph (224kph) top speed was no longer outstanding.

This, in fact, was just as Porsche wanted it to be, for the

Boxster was meant to signal a fresh start, the best possible 'entry-level' Porsche machine for a new century – and it was also a car about which the management did not want, nor expect, to hear criticisms. Complaints would certainly follow the Boxster's launch, but they were rarely about its function, its appearance, or its price. Mutterings about the need for more performance and equipment would be settled in future years as the options list built up.

Launched only three years after the last of the old-style 911s (the 993 model of 1993), the Boxster looked similar in many ways, though Porsche-watchers would soon learn to love (or occasionally hate) the complex shape of the new headlamps, the twin safety roll hoops behind the high-back seats, and the obvious resemblance, from any or all angles, to recent 911s of the early 1990s.

Although it was by no means a simple machine (service, particularly of the engine, would need the same specialised attention as ever) this car was going to set new Porsche standards and introduced new owners to the marque. Big

**BOXSTER
SPECIFICATION**

ENGINE
Flat 6

CAPACITY
2480 cc

BORE X STROKE
86 x 72mm

COMPRESSION RATIO
11.0:1

POWER
204bhp

VALVE GEAR
Double overhead camshafts,
four valves per cylinder

FUEL SYSTEM
Bosch Motronic engine
management, and fuel injection

TRANSMISSION
Five-speed manual, or optional
five-speed automatic

FRONT SUSPENSION
Independent, by MacPherson
struts, coil springs, telescopic
dampers, anti-roll bar

REAR SUSPENSION
Independent, by MacPherson
struts, coil springs, telescopic
dampers, anti-roll bar

BRAKES
All discs

WHEELS
Five bolt alloy

WEIGHT
2756lb (1250kg)

MAXIMUM SPEED
139mph (224kph)

YEARS IN PRODUCTION
Introduced in 1996, still in
production

wheels and tyres, combined with long-travel suspension promised a soft ride, the power-assisted steering provided an easy time in traffic, while the anti-lock brakes were well up to Porsche standards.

But, in view of recent Porsche advances, would 204bhp be enough, and would it be good value ? First impressions, backed up by road tests were that it would, if the original price levels could be maintained.

Autobahn cruising was still possible at 120mph and more, one could sprint up to 100mph in 18 seconds (rear-engined 911s would have been proud of this figure only 10 – 15 years earlier) while at the same time, day-to-day fuel economy figures of 27 or even 30mpg were clearly possible. More than this, was the fact that the Boxster was self-evidently such a practical open-top two-seater. With fully-trimmed luggage compartments at front *and* rear, with a transverse rear spoiler which rose eagerly to do its stabilising duty at 50mph and more, and with the first truly modern, well-laid and user-friendly facia/instrument display for more than

two Porsche decades, it could only be a winner.

And so it was. Demand was such that Porsche had to buy in additional assembly capacity from a specialist in Finland. For the 2000 Model Year they hastened to introduce a 3.2-litre/252bhp Boxster S, and at the same time the 'basic' Boxster became a 2.7-litre/220bhp machine.

Progress ? There was going to be a lot of this in the next decade.

911 CARRERA (Type 996)

In launching an all-new 911 in 1997, Porsche was taking the biggest gamble of its existence. The original 911, previewed as long ago as 1963, had been the backbone of Porsche's business for more than 30 years. The big question now was would seasoned Porsche customers take to an entirely different type of car ?

It needed only a few moments of study to realise that the new-generation 911 was much changed from previous sports cars of that pedigree. Apart from sharing much front-end engineering with the Boxster (the two cars had 36 per cent commonality, a figure which made company cost accounts smile happily), the new model (Project Code '996' in Stuttgart language) was a complete breakaway from the long-established theme.

The miracle was that Porsche had made the new car look so very much like the old - yet it had been updated in every respect. The basic profile remained – low-snout, 2 + 2 seating, and long sweeping tail, with a flat-six engine tucked within it - but every single component was newly-engineered.

The fact that the new car was longer, wider, heavier, smoother and more driver-friendly was immediately obvious, as was its definite but under-emphasised 'softer' character, with a thoroughly modern facia, instrument panel and driving position. Here was a car which had grown longer by more than 7in (185mm), yet miraculously it was 110lb (50kg) lighter than before. Although the new engine was 213cc smaller, it was 28bhp more powerful. Even the weight distribution was subtly more favourable than before - only 61 per cent of the bulk was over the rear wheels.

A bit more determined digging was required, though, to see that the 24-valve, 3.4-litre, twin-cam flat-six was a water-cooled design (a derivative of the Boxster's power unit, which had been introduced only a year earlier), to learn that this was a much more rigid body shell than before, and to realise that this was a truly modern and integrated layout. It included automatic air conditioning, exceptional handling – as usual bomb-proof and corrosion-proof, guaranteed by a lengthy construction warranty.

From the nose to the windscreen/front bulkhead, including the entire front suspension and power-assisted steering installation, the new '996' 911 shared all its parts with the Boxster, but the layout was fresh. In the traditional 911 manner, the engine was still behind the line of the rear wheels, with the six-speed transmission ahead of it,

169

though the multi-link rear suspension (mounted on an alloy sub-frame, and with many aluminium members) was also based on that of the Boxster.

Nothing seemed to have been forgotten, and nothing taken for granted. Wheels and tyres were even larger than before - with 255/40ZR17in rubber at the rear, this made the early 1960s 911 tyres of 165-15 look like bicycle equipment - and even bigger, 18in wheels, were also optional. The massive brakes had been subject to enormously demanding development testing – 25 successive slows to 60mph from 90 per cent of top speed, without showing any signs of fade. For the first time, electronic traction control was also available – but for the brave driver there was the facility to switch this off.

With a more spacious cab than before, and with styling which was smoother, more '2000s' than '1980s', this Porsche had a less aggressive appearance and was surely a car at the start of a long development cycle. When critics suggested that it was a shade more 'Grand Touring' than 'Sports Coupé', Porsche directors merely smiled politely, and flipped happily through their order books.

Because Porsche was determined to make its mark with the new-generation 911, there was virtually no overlap with the old. Although derivatives like the old Turbo continued for another season, the new 'entry-level' 911 took over smoothly, directly and totally at once. The last of the old types were built in mid-1997, while the first of the '996' followed in the autumn of that year - the transformation being brisk, surgical, and successful.

When the first cars were delivered, and released for press

With a more spacious cab than before, and with styling which was very much smoother, more '2000s' than '1980s', this Porsche had a less aggressive appearance and was surely a car at the starting point of a long development cycle.

road tests, their change of character was clear. If one could describe a 173mph/300bhp car as 'softer' than before, then this surely was such a machine - easier to drive, more comfortable to live with on long journeys, yet still capable of returning 20 – 22mpg and more.

By any standard measurements, the new car was a big jump ahead of the old - in refinement, in reliability, in comfort, and in straight-line performance. So seamless was the acceleration that is was easy to recall that 300bhp had been a ground breaking *turbocharged* output at Porsche only two decades earlier.

Whingers – and, amazingly, there were a few – suggested that this 911 had somehow 'gone soft', but Porsche took this as a compliment, concluding that it indicated that their goals of providing a more peaceful combination of straight line performance, a soft ride, cabin silence, and heavy-traffic flexibility had all been reached.

Measured purely as a sports car, the 911 was still an exhilarating package. So what if the 173mph top speed could not legally be enjoyed on many of the planet's open roads? There was still the joy of reaching 100mph from rest in a blink of no more than 10 seconds, or of breaching British and North American speed limits from rest, in less than six seconds.

Sensual delights included the ability to change up from second to third gear at 72mph - knowing that there were three more changes to go, and that 72mph was already at or above the speed limit in many so-called civilised nations ! All of which could be achieved in true comfort. It was cool in the hottest weather likely to be found in the USA's southern states (where many 911s would certainly be sold) and comfortable and safe in the unfriendly winters of Northern Europe.

The handling, too, was an advance on the old. Front and rear suspensions both featured MacPherson struts. Not only that, but careful development also provided very sophisticated control of wheel movements and attitudes. The result was a pleasing combination, and a car that would no longer understeer ferociously when the driver wanted to change direction, or try to swap ends if he lost heart in mid-corner.

And this, in 1997, was only the beginning. If Porsche continued to develop the design in their own inimitable way, what further advances could be expected in the next few years?

911 CARRERA (TYPE 996) SPECIFICATION

ENGINE
Flat 6

CAPACITY
3387cc

BORE X STROKE
96 x 78mm

COMPRESSION RATIO
10.4:1

POWER
296bhp

VALVE GEAR
Double overhead camshafts, four valves per cylinder

FUEL SYSTEM
Bosch Motronic engine management, and fuel injection

TRANSMISSION
Six-speed manual

FRONT SUSPENSION
Independent, by McPherson struts, coil springs, telescopic dampers, anti-roll bar

REAR SUSPENSION
Independent, by multi-links, coil springs, telescopic dampers, anti-roll bar

BRAKES
All discs

WHEELS
Five bolt alloy

WEIGHT
2911lb (1320kg)

MAXIMUM SPEED
173mph (278kph)

YEARS IN PRODUCTION
Introduced in 1997, still in production

911 TURBO

The wait had been worthwhile. After the launch of the new-generation water-cooled 911 of 1997, it took two full years before Porsche was ready to introduce the turbo-charged version. There were no disappointments, for under the same skin as the new '996' 911, the chassis was an advance on anything which had gone before. All this, and a massively impressive 420bhp engine, made this a great new Porsche.

Planning its specification had been straightforward enough. On the one hand, there were the traditions of the old-model 911 Turbo to uphold – this being a car which had finally had 408bhp, and Porsche's latest four-wheel-drive installation – while on the other, there was the ultra-capable basis of the new 911 chassis, engine and body shell of the new generation cars.

Inspection showed that yet again the German engineers had lavished great care and infinite pains on a new model. It wasn't just that the new chassis had been refined, or that the water-cooled engine had been made yet more flexible, but features as distinct as the brakes and the styling, the ride height and the choice of transmissions had all been improved.

Structurally, of course, the 911 Turbo was nearly identical to the four-wheel-drive version of the 911 (the Carrera 40 which had been introduced in 1998), but there were dozens of mechanical up-grades – and one huge difference. Here, for the first time, was a turbocharged version of the new-generation water-cooled engine, which showed off the enormous amount of development potential that had always been built in.

Visually it was easy enough to pick the new Turbo from its normally-aspirated relatives. The stylists had chosen yet another variation of slanting, complex shape of headlamp, the wheels and tyres were the biggest and fattest yet (18in diameter wheels were specified), there were subtle wheel arch flares at the rear, combined with air intakes for the intercoolers - and of course there was a two-level transverse spoiler across the tail.

It was under the skin, though, that the innovations were so exciting. At 3,600cc, with the same bore and stroke, there seemed to be similarities to older Porsche units, but this was superficial, as the latest 420bhp turbo-power came from the largest version of the new water-cooled unit which had already been seen in the modern-generation Boxster and 911 types.

With twin overhead-camshafts per bank, four valves per cylinder, twin turbochargers (one serving each bank of three cylinders), and twin intercoolers, each tucked into the bodywork behind each rear wheel, this was a phenomenal engine in which the boost arrived at a very low speed and hung on throughout the range. Peak torque was developed at a mere 2,700rpm, at which point maximum boost was 27psi/1.85 Bar.

Not only was this colossal powerhouse linked to the latest six-speed manual transmission and four-wheel-drive, but for the very first time on a Turbo there was the option of Tiptronic 'S' five-speed automatic transmission. Depending on road conditions, tyre grip and driving methods, the front wheels conveyed up to 40 per cent of engine power, the whole being controlled by Porsche's new PSM (Porsche Stability Management) system. Typically, due to its electronic wizardry, and with sensors like those used in the ABS braking system, the monitored wheel grip, could even apply individual brakes at individual wheels and, *in extremis*, could also send electronic messages to the engine management system to reduce engine power.

This new power train, alone, would have been enough to deliver a magnificent, extremely safe car, but Porsche went several stages further. Not only was the body shell set slightly closer to the ground than before, but the wheels were enlarged, with extremely fat (295/30 section at the rear) tyres and wider rims were also standardised. Suspension settings had all been re-assessed. Cross-drilled and vented brake discs were larger, and there would also be

an optional extra of ceramic-material discs too.

All in all, this was the sort of specification which prompted grown men to sit down carefully, dig out their wallets and bank books, and wonder why they could not immediately order a new 911 Turbo, there and then. By almost any standards, this looked like the most versatile, fastest Porsche road-car yet launched, for with a claimed top speed of 189mph/305kph it was already one of the fastest cars in the world. It could sprint from rest to 100mph in less than ten seconds, cruise at more than 150mph whenever and wherever the law allowed, and still have a great deal of performance in reserve.

But that was not all. The new 911 Turbo was the sort of package that seemed to have thought of everything, then improved on it. Turbocharged or not, the engine was extremely flexible, and very driveable. The Tiptronic 'S' transmission had two modes — fully automatic or what

Visually it was easy enough to pick the new Turbo from its normally-aspirated relatives. The stylists had chosen yet another variation of slanting, complex shape of headlamp, the wheels and tyres were the biggest and fattest yet (18in diameter wheels were specified), there were subtle wheel arch flares at the rear, combined with air intakes for the intercoolers - and of course there was a two-level transverse spoiler across the tail.

new rear-engined chassis could be. Maybe it wasn't as noisy as before, and maybe it wasn't as untamed – but it was an all-round better car.

People who had complained when the old-type Turbo was killed off in 1998/1999 soon learned their error. The Turbo was back.

many liked to call the F1 'steering wheel button' option, where the driver could change gear for himself, while not needing to use a clutch.

Up front there were huge air intakes, which would have been dramatic without a function to perform - but they did that too, for the engine cooling radiators were right behind them. As with other modern cars, the specification was littered with acronyms, for in addition to ABS and PSM, on the Tiptronic transmission there was also ETM (Electronic Transmission Management) which automatically matched gear change points to the perceived method of driving! With automatic air conditioning, electrically adjustable seats, a leather interior trim, a trip computer, electric opening of engine and luggage compartment lids, and more, and more, this was an extremely well-equipped package.

More than anything, of course, there was the new car's performance – blisteringly fast in a straight line, safe and secure in twisty conditions, and as well-balanced as the

911 TURBO (1999)
SPECIFICATION

ENGINE
Flat 6

CAPACITY
3600cc

BORE X STROKE
100 × 76.4mm

COMPRESSION RATIO
9.4:1

POWER
420bhp

VALVE GEAR
Double overhead camshafts, four valves per cylinder

FUEL SYSTEM
Bosch DME engine management system, fuel injection, and twin turbochargers

TRANSMISSION
Six-speed manual, or five-speed Tiptronic automatic transmission, with permanent four-wheel-drive

FRONT SUSPENSION
Independent, by double wishbones, coil springs, telescopic dampers, anti-roll bar

REAR SUSPENSION
Independent, by double wishbones, coil springs, telescopic dampers, anti-roll bar

BRAKES
All discs

WHEELS
Five bolt alloy

WEIGHT
3396lb (1540kg)

MAXIMUM SPEED
189mph (305kph)

YEARS IN PRODUCTION
Introduced in 1999, still in production

INDEX